MY FAVO...

ANGEL STORIES

JOE L. WHEELER

Pacific Press®
Publishing Association

Nampa, Idaho | Oshawa, Ontario, Canada
www.pacificpress.com

Cover designed by Gerald Lee Monks
Cover illustration by Marcus Mashburn
Inside design by Kristin Hansen-Mellish

Scripture quotations marked NLT are taken from the
Holy Bible, New Living Translation, copyright © 1996,
2004. Used by permission of Tyndale House Publishers,
Inc., Wheaton, Illinois 60189. All rights reserved.

Scriptures quoted from NKJV are from The New King
James Version, copyright © 1979, 1980, 1982, Thomas
Nelson, Inc., Publishers.

Scripture quotations from *The Message*. Copyright © by
Eugene H. Peterson, 1993, 1994, 1995, 1996, 2000,
2001, 2002. Used by permission of NavPress Publishing Group.

Additional copies of this book are available by calling
toll-free 1-800-765-6955 or by visiting
www.adventistbookcenter.com.

www.joewheelerbooks.com

Representing the author is WordServe Literary Group
Ltd., 10152 Knoll Circle, Highland Ranch, CO 80130.

Library of Congress Cataloging-in-Publication Data:

Wheeler, Joe L., 1936-
  My favorite angel stories / Joe L. Wheeler.
    pages cm
  ISBN 13: 978-0-8163-5019-3 (pbk.)
  ISBN 10: 0-8163-5019-1 (pbk.)
1. Angels—Christianity. 2. Miracles. I. Title.
BT966.3.W44 2013
235'.3—dc23
                                              2013039100

13 14 15 16 17 • 5 4 3 2 1

DEDICATION

They are two of the dearest people I know. She has gone through life as excited as a small child with this wonderful world we share. In fact, as a teenager, she devoured every page of the family encyclopedia set. Even today, so many years later, traveling with her is an adventure, as she wants to explore every unknown side road she sees. Her husband, as a pilot, is in love with the air, as well as her. He is also committed to mission life and to serving those less fortunate wherever they may be. Supposedly, they are now retired—but you wouldn't know it by watching them serve. Thus, it gives me great joy to dedicate this book of angel stories to my sister-in-law and brother-in-law, who are responsible for two of the stories in this collection.

Marla and Gary Marsh
of
Poplar, Montana

CONTENTS

INTRODUCTION

IS THERE A DIFFERENCE BETWEEN BIBLICAL AND NEW AGE ANGEL STORIES?

As I drove down Conifer Mountain one golden September morning, with here and there, small splotches of yellow aspen leaves announcing the imminence of another seasonal change, my mind was on another subject: I was breathing a prayer to my writing Partner, the good Lord: *Lord, I'm in a quandary. The deadline for this book of angel stories is upon me, and I still don't have the foggiest idea as to how I ought to organize the stories, which story should have placement precedence, and what my introduction should be about. Oh, of course it will be about angels, but that's such a broad subject that I'm still at sea. What aspect of the ministry of angels should I develop in the introduction? Would You, once again, permit me to access Your deep wisdom wells? Mine are so shallow and inadequate for today's demands.*

As I walked into the café for our weekly Conifer service club breakfast, little did I know that the Lord was already in the process of answering my prayer. Invariably, our club sessions conclude with what we call "Happy Dollars," as each member responds to the question, "Why are you happy today?" With the answer, each respondent tosses out two dollar bills as a contribution to our club expenses. Almost always, this part of our morning hour begins at 8:20 (ten minutes before we conclude the meeting). But for some unexplainable reason, one of our members threw out his two dollars a half-hour early, and the others quickly followed.

As for me, I declared that I was happy because of the manuscript of angel stories I was working on. Immediately, one member pounced: "How do you know when you have a *real* angel story? Might it not be that they are merely stories of coincidence?" In the crossfire discussion that followed, another variable came up: the difference between an "angel" story and one that would be compatible with angels portrayed in the Bible. How did I differentiate between the two?

Fortunately, I'd already done spade work on these questions, even though I hadn't specifically addressed them in my earlier angel books. In this case, I'd been impressed to take a time-consuming side trip: scan through around a dozen angel story collections in my library and ascertain whether they were all compatible with scriptural angels. Even though these books were all put out by Christian publishers, it didn't take me long to discover that there was no norm.

I'd already been jarred by a firsthand account written by a Christian minister, having to do with one memorable May day when, while taking a walk with his wife, suddenly, they heard talking approaching them from behind. Whoever it was, they were moving faster than they, so they slowed to let them pass. But, what should they then behold but angels in flowing garments floating through the skies above the transfixed couple: feminine angels animatedly speaking in an unknown language. There was no apparent reason for why these angels chose to reveal themselves to the couple, unless it was to prove to the watchers that angels actually existed. This first jar for me had to do with the gender of the angels: overtly feminine. The sec-

ond: that there was no apparent reason for their revelation to the watching couple.

Now that I was comparing angel stories within these angel story anthologies, I deliberately searched for stories depicting overtly female angels. Androgynous angels, I didn't count as a problem. Imagine my surprise to discover that there were quite a few collections that featured female angels. Then I discovered that they were invariably in collections put together by specific editors/compilers. Once I discovered that, I began looking for other aspects that jarred me; and I found them. I discovered that such stories tended to be *mystical, incorporating children portrayed as angelic, spiritualistic,* and *bordering on angel-worship.* Metaphorically, they made my hackles rise.

So now, I did a study on biblical angels. In over 250 biblical portrayals, none of them are feminine, but all masculine. Even Billy Graham confirms this. Furthermore, biblical angels are all business; they aren't just playing around or cutesy. The great battle between the forces of good and evil permits no flippancies or humanizing such as is depicted in Frank Capra's creation, Clarence, in *It's a Wonderful Life.* Scriptural angels don't merely saunter in, but rather there is invariably a serious reason for their being there, whether or not the humans in the account know for sure what that danger might be. When in a life or death countdown, they bark orders like a drill sergeant!

How grateful I was, in our discussion, that I now knew the difference between the scriptural angel stories and New Age angel stories—I hadn't, only a week before.

By now, our club members, when the official meeting time was over, got into serious discussion as to what I looked for in choosing angel stories I felt comfortable with. I answered that I excluded stories that were merely coincidental. There had to be deviation from natural law. Immediately, one member said, "Give us an example!"

I chose one of the stories I'd heard my father-in-law tell, taken from his own life story. Since Kirby Palmer, my brother-in-law, heard it told more than his sisters had, I asked for his text—and it had just arrived. So, in condensed form, I told them the story titled "The Turning Point." Once I finished, there was a veritable explosion of somewhat similar accounts that actually took place in the lives of those present.

Chuck told of a time when he was young, evidencing more testosterone than brains (typical of males of a certain age), and was roaring down a two-lane road on his motorcycle in California's Mojave Desert. Speed: ninety-five to one hundred miles per hour. For some unexplainable reason, several times he felt an invisible hand pushing him into the opposite lane. He just couldn't make sense of it. Suddenly, right after the hand had shoved his motorcycle into the opposite lane, there in the blur of speed to his right was a large plank stretching across the lane he should have been in. Had he been in that lane, at the speed he was traveling, he never could have missed it. And he'd have been dead. He *knew* God had sent an angel to spare his life!

And then another member, Ron, spoke up, saying, "It's amazing: my story is almost a mirror image of the one Joe just shared with us. And I was about the same age: a boy doing stupid things." And he proceeded to tell us of how the local sheriff had twice arrested him for driving a motorcycle without a license (he was too young to get one); the second time, he'd been sternly warned that if it happened again, he'd be thrown in jail. So he sold his Triumph motorcycle and instead bought an ancient truck (the only four-wheeled vehicle he could afford) and drove it without a license, even knowing what would happen to him if he were caught for the third time. He'd traded his Triumph for a piece of land in Colorado's foothills—turned out that it was in such a remote area that no roads could get to it. So he decided to load up his sorry excuse for a truck with gravel and haul it in to his new property and begin to create graveled access to it.

Well, his truck went slower and slower as it steamed up into the foothills. Finally, he reached what passed for a turn-off (little more than a wide trail), and the truck labored slower and slower yet until he drove it onto a small bridge—and there in the middle of it, it stopped, unable to go any farther. And as if that wasn't bad enough, the truck full of gravel was so heavy that the bridge broke, and he and the truck crashed through into a ravine.

Now, he *was* in a pickle! In those days, this was still wild country—human habitations few and far between, almost no traffic on the dirt road, and none whatsoever on this trail that masqueraded as a road. He was a long, long way from home. He didn't dare contact the law, even if he could have found an officer in the wilds of Coal Creek Canyon. So he prayed, "Lord, as You well know, I've got myself into a lot of predicaments before, but this has got to be the stupidest one yet. I haven't the slightest idea as to what to do. But if You ever were going to get me out of a jam, this would sure be an awfully good one to choose."

Then, unbelievably, he looked up, hearing a truck. *Where in the world did it come from?* The driver got out and yelled, "You have any idea where I can buy some gravel?"

Ron, half laughing, pointed to the gravel in the back of his truck, and said, "As you can see, I can sell you some; this is too heavy a load for my truck to pull at this elevation. But, before I sell it to you, you'd first have to figure out how to get my truck out of the ravine."

The driver of the truck declared that he felt he could extricate the truck, but they'd first need to lighten up Ron's truck. So, after transferring much of the travel and getting paid for it, and hauling Ron's now lighter truck out of the ravine, Ron thanked his rescuer and made it up to his new property. Ron never saw him again, nor did he ever find anyone else who had. First of all, how did he happen to appear on that wide trail so far from the main road? And to strain the laws of probability even further: be looking for gravel? The only possible answer: It *had* to be an angel.

Other similar angel stories were told—by this time, we'd run over our regular meeting time by a full half hour.

The only possible conclusion I can come to is this: When each of us looks back over our lives, rare will be the person who doesn't see incidents like these, providential rescues, times when our lives were spared by unexplainable deviations from natural law and natural probabilities, when God stepped in, through His angels, to save us.

By the time I returned home from that morning's service club meeting, the Lord had answered all the questions in my early morning prayer. ❧

—*Joseph Leininger Wheeler*

SECTION ONE

"When they call on me, I will answer;
I will be with them in trouble.
I will rescue them and honor them."
Psalm 91:15 (NLT)

*N*othing was harder, in putting together these angel stories, than deciding which story should anchor the collection—reason being that there are so many powerful stories to choose from. Believing as I do that there are no great authors, only great stories, who a given author happens to be is almost irrelevant: it is the power of the story itself that determines placement.

In the end, what decided the issue was the title itself, for in a unique way, a book title bears on its back, for better or worse, all the other stories in a collection. If it isn't almost perfect as a choice, it discounts all the other story inclusions.

And I'll have to admit there is a personal reason for my choice: One of the dearest people I've known in my lifetime is my late father-in-law, Derwood Palmer, who made such an impact on the lives of all those who knew him. Quite candidly, I was curious about what it was that shaped him, gave him his patented one-of-a-kind slant on life, and set the shape of his sails. And this my brother-in-law, Kirby, provided, out of the recesses of his memory.

And I've always been intrigued with turning points. Such epiphanies more often than not are experienced unnoticed; only in retrospect, as you look back through a life, do you stumble on days that, for one reason or another, were pivotal: if they had never been, how different that life might have been.

The Turning Point

Kirby Palmer

It was beginning to look like disaster for the seventeen-year-old boy.
Unwanted at home, out of money, and stranded in the Trinity Alps!
What should he do?

My father, Derwood Palmer, was one of the most fascinating men I ever met: contractor, builder, brick mason, missionary, teacher, musician, raconteur, and an irresistible funny man—life in his vicinity was never boring.

But it wasn't always so. His mother having died at his birth, he became a foster child. His foster brothers and sisters treated him as an unwelcome intruder, and his foster father not only made him feel unwelcome, he pointed to a nearby pile of scrap lumber and told him to build a shed for himself in the backyard and live there instead of in the house with the rest of the family.

Though he attended church with his foster family, there was so much disconnect between what was preached from the pulpit and how he was treated by supposed Christians that Dad wanted no part of it. Loving music

as he did, and having a great ear for melody (hear a piece once; he could usually play it), he started playing in bars for the fun of it, as well as the small income it brought him. He started smoking as well.

When about seventeen, he decided to go to north-central California to pick almonds during harvesttime. While working in the almond orchards, he noticed a very old automobile. He made an offer for it, and the rancher accepted it. Working on it during off-hours, by the time the almonds had all been picked, he'd managed to get the old car in working order so he'd have transportation to go home.

But, en route home, it didn't take him long to discover that his ancient jalopy had a rather disgusting habit of stopping dead in its tracks every twenty to thirty miles, for no obvious reason. In about twenty to thirty minutes, it would start up again, whether he worked on it or not.

Occasionally, he'd pick up a hitchhiker, but they'd each and all abandon him when the perverse auto would stop again in the middle of the road.

One of the characteristic traits of my father was his keen eyesight. Because of it, he was able to see items such as tools and other odds and ends along the road that no one else would notice. Thus it was on this start-and-stop, start-and-stop trip, he made an unforced stop to pick up what turned out to be a .22-caliber pistol. He quickly wrapped it up in a piece of cloth and placed it under the seat. The road being empty at the time, there were no witnesses.

Another disgusting habit his reluctant steed had was that it got terrible mileage. Every time he filled it, the gas disappeared so fast he eventually got out to see if there was a big hole in the gas tank. What filled him with ever more apprehension was that all these stops at gas stations were draining his summer savings at an alarming rate.

Eventually, he reached Redding and turned west on 299 toward his home in Eureka. As the cycle continued: constant dying of the car, cranking the engine (The older vintage autos had no starter on the dashboard; you had to get out, walk to the front of the car, and hand crank it until the engine caught fire, so to speak. Many were the hands and arms that were broken in those days, when the crank backfired on you.), and the constant need for more gas.

It wasn't long, as the car labored along climbing into the Trinity Alps, before the inevitable happened: the car stopped once again; but this time there was no more money to buy gas with! And this was a good thirty years before credit cards came in and one could buy things without having the money to pay for them.

So, what to do now? His summer savings were gone. It was a lonely dirt road back then, with very little traffic on it. He was far away from what passed for home—with no way to get there.

For the first time in his life, he knew desperation. He now recalled what he'd been taught in his foster home: the power of prayer. Round and round the contrasting thoughts churned in his head—his hurt at being unwanted and unappreciated versus what he'd learned about God. Finally, seeing no other alternative, there on the deserted dusty road, he turned to God and prayed for help and forgiveness.

Suddenly, he looked up and saw a horseman riding toward him. As the rider reached the stalled car, he drew rein, and asked my father if he had a gun for sale.

Startled, Dad replied, "Yes, I have a .22-caliber pistol."

After looking it over, the horseman offered fifty dollars for it.

Dad agreed on the price—he'd have taken far less in his extremity—reached in his pocket for the wallet, placed the fifty dollars in it, and looked up to thank the rider.

But there was no horse, no rider, no gun. Yet, when he rechecked the wallet, there was the money the rider had given him! He shook his head in disbelief. He looked down at the road where the horse had stood during his dialogue with the rider. There were tracks leading up to the place where the horse had stopped—*but there were no tracks leading away from there*!

Dad then thanked God for the miracle on his behalf, for making it possible for him to make it back to Eureka. He then walked and walked till he reached a gas station, borrowed a gas can and filled it, and was driven by the gas station worker to the car, put the gas in the tank, drove to the gas station, filled the tank, and then drove the remaining seventy-five miles home.

Dad never forgot how God sent an angel on horseback to him, sold a gun he hadn't had with him when he left the almond orchards to the angel (who clearly didn't need it!). Most importantly, that experience resulted in an instant rebuilding of Dad's shattered self-esteem. Though he was neither wanted nor loved at home, he was so important to the Creator of this world that He sent an angel to rescue him.

For my father, *that was the turning point of his life.* ❧

*I*n all the years I've searched through archival story digs, as a story archaeologist, W. A. Spicer's 1918 tour de force, The Hand That Intervenes, *is without question the greatest collection of angel stories I've ever come across. Not because they are powerfully crafted in a literary sense, but because of the sheer amount of work represented by Spicer's attempts to corral in one book the most moving angel stories ever written. And they are drawn from the story archives of many Christian denominations.*

It was after reading this old story, for the second time, that the real message of the story was driven home to me: that God does not generally act on platitudes or generalities, but rather to specifics. As I thought back over my own prayer life over the years, I couldn't help but wince, remembering that so many of my prayers are so broad and indefinite that, in retrospect, they often seem like buckshot prayers (the hunter, doubting he can hit anything with a single bullet, turns instead to a shotgun, hoping that something in all the particles will hit something). In fact, I'd been praying a certain prayer for some time in just that way. So impressed was I with this story that I now prayed for a specific outcome; then realizing it would probably take some time before I knew the outcome, prayed that God would also let me know right away when the issue was resolved.

What a faith strengthener for me it was when, within forty-eight hours, here came an out-of-the-blue e-mail notifying me that the issue was now being resolved, thereby answering both prayers at once!

FIREWOOD AND CANDLES

W. A. Spicer

" 'O Father, we've got some wood and some candles!' "
" 'Where did you get them? Are you sure they were not left here by mistake?' "
So what did bring them? And why?

The following account of an experience in old-time New England was reported in a contemporary paper called *The Reflector*.

"An upright man, Deacon P——, was financially ruined by endorsing the note of a man whom he trusted. With a dying wife and children, he was forced to seek other employment in midwinter. One morning, when his resources were gone and no work had been found, his little girl reported that the wood and the candles were gone; 'and how shall we take care of dear mother tonight?' she asked her father.

"He fled to his closet, and there, in an agony of prayer, besought the Lord for help; and forgetting all other wants, pled and pled again for the two articles now specially needed, specifying them with reiterated earnestness. He arose from his knees in full as-

surance of faith and with heavenly tranquility, and went forth expecting deliverance, looking for it, however, in but one way: through his own earnings.

"But after a fruitless day of seeking employment, gloomily he returned home. He entered his gate and was startled to see before him a generous pile of wood. Little Johnny opened the door, clapping his hands, exclaiming, 'O Father, we've got some wood and some candles!'

" 'Where did you get them? Are you sure they were not left here by mistake?'

" 'O no, Father,' interrupted Hatty, 'they were not left by mistake. A man knocked at the door with his whip, and when I opened it, asked if you lived here. I told him you did. Then he said, "Here are some candles, and a load of wood for him." I asked him if you sent him, and he said, "I rather guess your father doesn't know anything about it." "Who did send them, then?" said I. "Oh," said he, "I mustn't tell. But you may say to your father, they are a present." '

"But to what instrumentality they were indebted for the relief was a mystery. And what particularly interested Deacon P—— was the character of the anonymous presents—that the very things so much needed, and no others, should be sent; and he was sure he had mentioned his need of them to no human ear.

"He questioned the children again. They described the man who knocked at the door, the horse and truck he drove. A new thought struck him. 'Why,' said he, 'that team belongs to my old enemy, Graff. Can it be possible that he is the donor? If so, surely the finger of God has touched his heart.' Deacon P—— was, however, so convinced that he was their benefactor, that he resolved on an immediate call on that gentleman."

This Mr. Graff, it seems, was a distiller. Once the two had been friends; but Deacon P—— had been so active in the temperance cause that he had earned the enmity of the distiller. Try as the deacon might to conciliate the man and to show that he had no personal hostility to him, the distiller had rudely refused to acknowledge the deacon's salutations. This was the man the deacon now called upon. The account continues:

"Deacon P—— entered the distillery of his old friend. For the first time in years its proprietor looked up with a nod of recognition. It was evident something unusual had softened his heart. 'I have called,' said the deacon, 'to ask if you can tell me who sent some wood and candles to my house today?'

" 'Yes, sir, I sent them.'

" 'You are very kind; but pray tell me how you came to do so.'

" 'But first let me inquire if you really needed them?'

" 'O, I cannot express to you how much!'

" 'Well, then, I suppose I must explain,' said Mr. Graff. 'It is all very singular, and sometimes seems very foolish.

" 'This morning, about ten o'clock, as I was busy at my work, suddenly a voice seemed to say to me, *Send some wood to Deacon P——; he is in want.* I was astonished. I tried to banish the thought, and went to work more earnestly. I could not believe you needed it. And I could not send it to you of all people. But the voice—it seemed to me—said again with painful distinctness, *Send some wood to Deacon P——, he is in want!* I rejected the idea as weak and silly, a mere phantasy of the brain; but it was of no use; I had to succumb. The more I ridiculed and fought it, the more vivid and irresistible was the impression, until to gain peace of mind, and in some awe, I bade John load his team with wood and leave it at your door.

" 'For a moment I was at rest; but only for a moment. The imperative whisper came, *Send some candles!* Said I to myself, This is too absurd, I will not gratify this whim; but again I was so beset with the mandate, and so distressed and baffled in repelling it, that as a cheap way to get out of torment, I handed John a package of candles also.

" 'This has been on my mind ever since. Sometimes I have thought it almost a freak of insanity, and then, again, such was the strange character of the impression, so unexpected, so solemn and powerful, and such the singular peace following compliance with its dictates, that I almost believe it to be supernatural.'

" 'It is, indeed, the doings of "Him who is wonderful in working," ' replied Deacon P——. 'It was about ten o'clock, I well remember, that I pled with God for the very articles you sent me, in an agony of wrestling I never knew before. It was then, too, that my soul was filled with the conviction that my prayer was heard, and relief would come.' " ❧

*I*t was eleven years ago that Kari Surdahl was impressed to send me this personal memory of a certain Christmas journey. In her letter of March 26, 2002, she noted that "Numerous people have been encouraging me to write it out for quite some time now. Last week, I felt impressed to do so. . . . It has never been told until now. The story is of a blizzard my mom and I were caught in over Christmas break from academy in 1977, and how the Lord saved us from being stranded, even frozen to death. . . . Two Christmases ago, you asked me to write it out and send it to you. I apologize for not getting it done until now. The Lord must have a use for it somewhere since I felt very impressed to get it done a few days ago."

Isn't it fascinating to discover how long a gestation period stories may have? Take this story: the author sat on it for twenty-three years before I asked her to write it out for me. She delayed writing it down for two more years, thus she missed my earlier angels story collection; thus in God's own timetable, it has been patiently waiting in our archives for eleven more years—and now, thirty-six years later, in God's "fullness of time," here it is!

You will discover it to be the second (after "The Turning Point") story in this collection to have the angel authentication resulting from tracks, or lack of them. Pay particular attention to the appearance, attire, personality, and so on, of the angels in these stories—some persist in not permitting anyone to see their faces clearly.

ANGEL IN THE DARKNESS

Kari Surdahl

There they were—a mother and her daughter—stranded in a fierce and bitterly cold blizzard. A flat tire, and not a lug nut could they loosen.
Surely they'd freeze to death when the last of the gas was used up. What should they do?

I can't see the road!" I squinted and blinked hard as I leaned forward, white knuckles clenching the wheel. The snow blew furiously across the road while large drifts piled up fast. Mom sat in the seat beside me as we made that December night journey in 1977 from Mount Ellis Academy to Rapid City, South Dakota. When we left Mount Ellis that evening on my Christmas break from school, we hadn't realized just how bad a storm we were heading into as we ventured from Montana out on the northern Wyoming plains.

"If only we could see the reflectors along the road!" Mom sounded worried as she scraped another thin layer of ice off the inside of the windshield. The Ford station wagon was needed for our large family, but for the two of us on this trip it seemed awfully big and cold. High winds and subzero temperatures forced their way through the seals of every nook and cranny despite the heater's attempts to keep it out. Our thermos of hot chocolate had long ago run out, and though bundled up as we were, I could feel my feet getting colder.

"We should have waited until . . ." Breaking the silence, I left the sentence unfinished as another blast of blowing snow and wind tried to push us off the road and into the blackness of the night. It approached midnight; and although neither of us voiced it, we realized that we hadn't seen another vehicle on the road in several hours. Suddenly, we felt very alone. The radio only produced static, so we had shut it off hours before. Besides, we couldn't have heard it over the howling of the blizzard outside anyway. I knew we were miles and miles from the nearest town and it would be a poor choice indeed to pull over and wait out the storm beside the road.

"Yes. I know," Mom tensely replied after a moment. "But I'm scheduled to work tomorrow night at the hospital. Had I known this storm would be this bad . . ." She, too, left her sentence unfinished. "What ifs" wouldn't do any good now. Another minute went by, and then she added, "When you see another road reflector or mile marker and can safely pull over to the edge without getting stuck, I would like us both to again ask for God's help and protection. We sure could use it just now!"

The blowing, swirling snow and wind came from nowhere only to pound on the car and disappear again into the unknown darkness. Although we could only manage about twenty miles per hour, I felt hypnotized into thinking we were going at least twice that fast. My wide open eyes grew dry and bloodshot from the strain of staring at the road, and the rest of my tense body was stiffening and going numb. *Is the howling of the wind getting louder and louder,* I wondered, *or am I imagining it?*

Our headlights penetrated the darkness hardly at all, just enough to reveal a complete whiteout. The last roadside reflector we had passed seemed to be at least a half mile behind us. Finding and staying on the road was a constant challenge. At times, with fear, I felt the left or right front tire edge off the road heading for the ditch, and I would have to steer in to find the road again.

"There's one!" Mom said eagerly, as I noticed her leaning forward and scraping the windshield to be certain it was a reflector she had seen. I eased up on the gas pedal, and we drifted to the shoulder of the road next to the metal post. We found a little comfort knowing that at some point another human had been there if only to install that post. Once the car stopped, the bone-chilling wind took away even the sound of the motor.

In the cold, Mom took my hand, and just before I closed my eyes, I saw her breath as she began to pray. "Our Father in heaven, we again pause to ask for Your protection on this perilous journey. We need to get home safely, and we put ourselves in Your care. I pray, Lord, that we will not have any car trouble and that this storm will pass quickly, and that You will give us safe passage home; nevertheless, not my will but Thine be done. I praise Your name for hearing and answering us; and I pray this all in Your name, amen." After I, too, had prayed, we felt comforted and smiled at each other.

I put the car in gear and was slowly beginning to edge back out on the road when another gust of wind loudly hit my side of the car. Feeling somewhat reassured from the momentary break, the eerie blasting of the wind somehow didn't seem quite as menacing as it had before. Mom didn't seem so tense now either; and as I looked over at her, she began to sing:

"Under His wings I am safely abiding;
Though the night deepens and tempests are wild,
Still I can trust Him; I know He will keep me;
He has redeemed me, and I am His child."

I joined Mom as she sang the chorus.

"Under His wings, under His wings,
Who from His love can sever?
Under His wings my soul shall abide,
Safely abide forever."

Although still in the midst of the storm, the questionable safety of our immediate future was lifted as though a great burden had been removed from our shoulders. We talked of other things while still keeping our eyes on where we guessed the road might lead.

Normally, Dad took us on this 1,100-mile round-trip journey back and forth to school at Mount Ellis Academy. But this time, work prevented him, and the duty fell to Mom, who drove up to get me. Mom never really enjoyed driving and tended to become drowsy behind the wheel on long trips. She preferred to be a passenger and had gladly agreed to allow me to drive. Having only just obtained my driver's license several months earlier, I lacked the experience to call upon in adverse driving conditions, despite the several years of driving farm equipment I had done for Frank King on the school's farm. Baling hay, summer fallowing, or harvesting grain was certainly different from trying to fight the wind in keeping the station wagon on the road during a severe winter blizzard, at night on a deserted highway.

Several more hours passed, and our visibility diminished even more. The speedometer needle indicated how slowly we crept along. I was unsure of how far we'd gone, but it felt like we'd been going forever. Mom had fallen asleep, and I tried to keep myself occupied as I remembered school, friends, and events. We'd just enjoyed our Christmas Banquet, where the school hired a team of horses with a sleigh to carry the couples in real style from the girls' dorm to the gym where the banquet was held. I smiled in the dark as I recalled the event.

B-A-N-G! Flop, flop, flop, flop!

Mom jolted awake in a panic. She grabbed the dashboard with one hand and the door with the other. "What was that?" she shrieked.

"*Oh no!* I think we just blew a tire!" I said in despair. Inching the steering wheel to the right, I tried to find the edge of the road. "I can't tell where the shoulder is! We've *got* to get over 'cause if another vehicle happens along, it'll hit us!"

"I'll get out and see if I can find the shoulder

of the road," Mom volunteered.

"OK," I hesitantly agreed. Worried for her safety, I added, "But only for just a minute. If we really do get stranded out here, we're going to need all the warmth we have left in us . . . And stay close to the car," I said somewhat sternly as she tried to open the door. The thought of Mom getting lost out in this blizzard frightened me. The crosswind slammed into the driver's side of the car, so Mom didn't have too much trouble getting her door open. The howling wind and snow immediately flooded the car as she climbed out into the night. Against the storm, she closed the door with much more difficulty.

Straining to keep my eyes on her, I watched her stagger in the gusting wind, as she looked for the side of the road. Then, through the dim headlights, I saw her motion me onto the shoulder. Seconds later, the door flung open, and the car again was filled with the loud flurry of wind and snow. Mom struggled with the door as she got in and collapsed in exhaustion from the bitter winds. It had taken a lot out of her. She didn't complain, but I could see that she was chilled to the bone. It wouldn't take long in this bitterly cold wind to be in serious trouble.

After taking an auto class from Dave Stanton at Mount Ellis Academy and learning from Frank King how, among other things, to repair equipment on the school's farm, I was confident in my ability to simply change a tire and cautiously eager to test my skills at a time when it really mattered. *But this is a little extreme!* I thought as I watched Mom vigorously rub her hands together for warmth. *There's no room for error. I can't fail Mom in this storm!*

"I think it's the right rear tire," I told her. "Do we have a spare tire with us?"

"I'm not sure," Mom said. "I think so. I always let Dad take care of the vehicles, and I trust he made sure we have what we need."

"What about the jack and star wrench? Are they where they should be?" Mom shrugged her shoulders. "Guess we'll find out," I said. "Why don't you stay here and I'll go check." Pulling down my knit hat and zipping up my coat as far as it would go, I tried to open the door. It was frozen shut, from either the ice or from the powerful wind. Removing my glove, I tried again. Fearful of breaking the handle, I decided to crawl over the seats to the back of the station wagon to try to find what we needed. Moving our luggage aside, I located and opened the hatch to the spare tire.

"All right! We have a good spare," I yelled above the howling wind.

"Thank You, Jesus!" faintly came my mother's words from the front seat.

Crawling back over the middle seat, I pulled the jack and wrench with me. "Do we have a flashlight?" I inquired. Opening the glove box, Mom found Grandpa's old flashlight and checked to see if it worked. The light flickered a bit before she shut it off and handed it to me. "I'll climb out the back door behind you, and you stay here and try to keep warm," I directed, ignoring the offer of help I knew was coming.

"But I really should come out and help you," she protested.

"You can help me by staying warm for now. If I have trouble and need you, I'll let you know." And with that I opened the door and jumped out as quickly as I could in order to keep the car as warm as possible.

The bitter cold and wind immediately took my breath away. Stumbling back to the flat tire, I knelt, put the flashlight under one arm, and pushed the snow out of the way in order to get the jack in place. In the darkness, the dim, flickering flashlight warned me that the batteries were nearly drained. I turned it off to conserve its remaining light and set it in the snow. I could hardly hear the car running as exhaust from the motor puffed in my face. In the blackness, I tested the jack to be sure I had it right, but it slipped and pinched my freezing fingers. Momentarily paralyzed, I gritted my teeth in pain. "Ouch" just didn't seem to be a strong enough word in those few seconds as I held my hand between my knees. Beginning to feel the sleep-inducing effects of carbon monoxide from the exhaust, I wondered when this would all be over.

Then I thought of Mom and wondered how she fared. *When I get this jack set under the car, I'll jump back in for a minute or two and warm up. . . . I'm already so cold,* I thought, *how am I ever going to get this tire changed without getting hypothermia?*

After checking on Mom and finding out that my smashed fingers were going to be all right, I fumbled my way back out through the snow as it piled up again on the passenger side. Already I had to kick the drifting snow away from my work area. Then, going around back, I had a tough time opening the tailgate in order to pull out the spare tire. The gusting wind was a great hindrance, so it was a real struggle to retrieve the tire. I placed it on the ground to sit on as I turned on the feeble flashlight in order to see as I tightened up the jack. The flashlight being of little use, I dropped it in the snow. By this time my fingers were starting to lose feeling; and since my toes hadn't been warm in the first place, they were now numb. *Just let me get these lug nuts loosened,* I told myself, *and then I'll go get warmed up again.*

Fitting the star wrench on the first lug nut, I attempted to loosen it. I strained as I twisted with all my might, but it would not break free. I braced the opposite end on the spare tire and slowly stepped up onto the wrench to use my weight to loosen it. Nothing. I began bouncing on it. Still, it held fast. *Oh dear! We're in big trouble!* I gasped for air into the wind. I tried another lug nut. And another.

And another. Not one would give up its hold.

I wondered how much gas we had left in the tank and doubted there was enough to last the night, much less get us to a gas station when this was all over. Many thoughts raced through my mind; some seemed pretty bleak. By then I wanted to cry, but the tears blew dry before they had a chance to well up. "There's no one for miles who even knows we're here, let alone who'd help us!" I mumbled with anxiety, squinting into the relentlessly unforgiving night as I pondered the sobering thought. *I'd better get back into the car before what little heat we have is unable to warm me back up.*

Maybe Mom has a good idea I haven't thought of, I said to myself as I let go of the wrench and climbed back into the warmth of the car. Pulling hard with my frozen fingers to shut the door, I locked the fearful blizzard outside. Mom turned around to look at me, handing me what little water we had left in our jug. I took the jug and a deep breath as she raised her eyebrows for a report.

"I can't get a single lug nut off," I said despairingly. "Getting one or two isn't enough, we have to get them *all*! And I can't even get one!" Then in a quiet tone mixed with fear, I slowly added, "I'm afraid we're stuck!"

Ignoring the storm, Mom calmly looked down for a moment in deep thought and then suddenly raised her head and said resolutely, "Come with me." She snuggled her winter clothes up tighter and opened the door.

"What?" I asked, puzzled.

Stepping out into the night, she yelled, "Come on!" As the howling wind carried her voice away, I scrambled for my door. Soon we stood by our troublesome tire, hunched against the biting wind. I looked at her for our next move.

"The Lord knows our desperate need at this time," she shouted into the wind. "Let's kneel down beside this flat tire and ask Him to help us."

Without another word, we knelt down together next to that rear passenger-side tire. I was chilled to the bone; but as Mom started to pray, a little warmth started to kindle inside me. The prayer that I so readily forgot a short time ago returned to my mind and I clutched on to it as our only hope. "Lord, please help us!" was all I managed to say.

As our prayer ended and we looked up, a set of bright headlights blinded our eyes. We could see the grill of a pickup truck as it pulled in behind us. Climbing to our feet, I heard Mom say, "Thank You, Lord!"

Bracing himself against the wind, a man who looked like a rancher held his hat on as he came around in front of his truck to see what was the matter. "How can I help?" he asked with head cocked into the wind and squinting from the icy sting of the driving snow. I told him of our dilemma as he sized up the situation for himself. Then he sat down on the spare tire as I had done, grabbed the wrench and effortlessly spun the lug nuts off the flat tire. In no time, he had the spare mounted and was tightening it down.

"How can we ever thank you?" Mom earnestly asked.

"Well," he said in a friendly tone that warmed our souls, "next time you see someone broken down by the side of the road, stop and lend a hand. I'd be much obliged."

"We sure will," Mom said emphatically as she helped me pick up the old tire, hoist it into the back of the station wagon, and maneuver it into place so I could lock it down.

Turning from the car to face this kind stranger, I said, "I really want to thank . . ." I stopped in midsentence. He was gone! Mom and I looked at each other, then to where he'd parked his pickup truck. It was gone too! Where did he go? In the short time it had taken us to put the old tire back into the car, there was no way he would have had time to get back to his truck and leave without either of us noticing it. No way! He had parked right behind us. We wandered around for a minute looking for his tracks. Nothing! We found no sign that he had ever been there!

Tears of thanksgiving and joy froze to our cheeks as we made our way back into the car. Thrilled, neither of us doubted now as to who had been there! It was an angel who had changed our tire. Our prayers for help had not been drowned out and lost by the howling of the relentless wind. Every word had reached the ear of our Savior.

No longer fearful of the storm outside the car, we started once again on our journey. Confident we would make it home safely, we tearfully sang for joy:

"Under His wings, O what precious
    enjoyment!
There will I hide till life's trials are o'er;
Sheltered, protected, no evil can harm me;
Resting in Jesus I'm safe evermore."

To this day, twenty-five years later, I am still encouraged with the remembrance that God never loses sight of His children, no matter where we are, no matter how dark the night!

*"He shall call upon Me, and I will
    answer him;
I will be with him in trouble;
I will deliver him and honor him."*

*"The angel of the LORD encamps all
    around those who fear Him,
And delivers them.
Oh, taste and see that the Lord is good;
Blessed is the man who trusts in Him!"*

—Psalms 91:15; 34:7, 8, NKJV ❧

*R*eaders who already have other story anthologies of ours will be aware that I mine old magazines for many of our stories. This one comes from one of the greatest family magazines ever published in America, The Youth's Instructor, *enduring over a hundred years.*

In this Elna English Mays story, you will discover that God's angels are tech-savvy too: enough to take control of a stopped car's electrical system, thereby saving the lives of three members of a family. You will note a number of other automobile-related stories in this collection.

The Master Controls the Switch

Elna English Mays

At first the snowflakes were light, but then they started to fall faster and faster, and the drifts grew deeper and deeper, and it got colder and colder in the convertible. Night fell. They saw no lights anywhere . . .

It was a happy family of Ziskas who joined hands for prayer just as the sun was sinking over the tops of the houses. In order to give the children a concrete example of the blessing and care of God, Mr. Ziska told of their own experience in earlier married life when God provided "shelter in the time of storm."

"Goodbye, Dad and Mom," Gerald called as he hurriedly slammed the car doors. Emily, his wife, and their little four-year-old son, Verne, were already settled in the front seat, waiting to leave the old farm.

Emily had carefully packed her jars in the rumble seat. Of course, the jars were filled with the delicious vegetables and fruits that they had gleaned from the big garden on the hill.

Verne waved his little chubby hand to his grandparents as the one-seated convertible rattled down the drive and onto the main road.

"Where are we going, Daddy?" Verne asked inquisitively. "Are we going to town, Daddy?"

"Yes, Verne, we are going to town to live for a long time."

During the summer, there was always plenty to do on the farm, but the winter was well under way, and the few chores to be done morning and evening did not warrant their help. Gerald was planning to find work in town. As the young family began their journey, beautiful white flakes of snow were sifting from the low gray clouds overhead. With his foot becoming heavier on the accelerator, Gerald smiled at his wife and young son. "This is quite a snowfall," he casually observed. "But if it gets very deep, we may wish we had borrowed Dad's chains."

Emily did not seem interested in the snow, much less in her husband's remarks. A whole new world had opened before her. She was admiring the trees that had been stripped of their leaves. She also noticed the frozen streams that only a few months before had been filled with sparkling water, but all the time she was thinking of the friends they would see again in town.

"It is almost unbelievable to think that we shall see Jack and Zella tonight. I hope we shall be able to find a nice little house near them," she remarked hopefully.

"Yes, it probably will be dark when we arrive. Perhaps they'll let us stay with them for the rest of the night."

Talking happily, the little family bounced along until they had passed the small towns of Spotted Horse and Wildcat. The snow continued to fall thicker and faster. The accompanying wind was mild at first, but in a matter of minutes, its increasing momentum could be felt rocking the car. A white phenomenon seemed to be blanketing the whole countryside at an unbelievable rate of speed.

"Emily, shall we stop at the next farmhouse to ensure our warmth and safety during the storm?"

"Yes, I will tell you if I see one on this side of the road, and at the same time you can be watching on that side."

Scraping unsteadily across the glass, the windshield wiper seemed to be struggling for breath. The car would not have benefited by a modern heater because the canvas top was covered with so many cracks it seemed as if the wind would tear it off.

"Daddy, I'm getting cold," complained little Verne as he snuggled closer to his father's side. The wind was howling fiercely by this time, and great gusts of snow blinded Gerald's vision, making it impossible for him to see the road. Becoming darker, the sky itself seemed to have opened above them and emptied the heavens of driving white flakes.

Slowly they battled the fierce storm. "Emily, am I on the road?" Gerald was calling as he leaned out the window, trying to keep the car away from the ledge at the very edge of the highway.

"You are going all right, but turn a little to the left—now, straight ahead. I still don't see a single house. It would be terrible to be out in these badlands all by ourselves and get stranded."

"Yes, dear, especially with Verne." Emily and Gerald were both chilled by the bitter cold, but their precious boy was now wrapped snugly in the comforter that was always in the car.

"Do you suppose we should turn around and try to get back to Wildcat?" asked Emily.

"I doubt if we could even get back now. The snow is drifting in great cliffs behind us."

The car chugged on and on through the blackness and terror of the blizzard. Emily, still watching eagerly for a farmhouse, was made dizzy by the swirling snow before her eyes. Verne had gone peacefully to sleep with the perfect trust that only a child can exemplify.

"Gerald, I am frightened! Will this never stop? Why did we choose a time like this to move? Do you suppose that God intends for us to perish in the deathly whiteness of this snow?"

Shaking with cold, Gerald suggested that their only hope was in prayer. He realized that they could not go on much longer. Stopping the car, he scooped the ice and snow off the windshield glass with his mittened hand. And before resuming the miserable spinning and crunching through those white barriers that loomed up before their eyes, he prayed, "Father, guide us to shelter, if it be Thy will." Then Emily prayed, "Jesus, help us not to doubt, but to have faith in Thy power."

After this petition there came to them a feeling of confidence and trust. This engulfed the husband and wife as they proceeded on their way.

By now, Emily was almost numb with the cold, but she was thinking little of her own comfort as she continued searching for a wayside house. Once in a while would she turn to see if Verne was all right.

"It is ten o'clock, Gerald. Do you have any idea where we are now?"

"No, but we ought to be coming to the farming section soon."

"It is getting so late that the farmers will have turned their lights out, and then it will be impossible to see the houses from the road."

"I only hope we are on the right road," said Gerald, putting the car in second gear to get through a huge drift.

Seeming not to hear him, Emily said, "Do you see a light in the distance?"

"Unless my eyes are deceiving me, I believe I do." Gerald tried to go a little faster, but speed was not at all possible.

"O Gerald, maybe it is someone else in the same predicament that we are experiencing. Does the light seem to be moving?" As they came closer, it was evident that the light was not moving. As they approached the dark object with its twin beams of light, Gerald was able to see the outline of a car. Stopping to see what the trouble might be, he found the car empty, with no sign of life in it. Just as he was about to get into his own car again, a shadow stretched vaguely before him in the falling snow. Alarmed, he quietly whispered to Emily that something was ahead of them. It was with mingled feelings of fear and anxiety that he again moved into the darkness.

"Wait a minute, stop—there it is!—the

farmhouse, it is right over there," Emily stammered.

Jumping out of the car, Gerald called back, "You stay here with Verne while I find out whether anyone lives in this house." Plunging through the deep snow, he stumbled around the house that looked miserably forsaken in the blackness and terror of the night. He mounted the steps and groped blindly for the door that jolted his hand to painful tingling as he knocked. A man opened the door, and the warmth from inside the house was soon melting Gerald's frosty eyebrows.

"We have come from Gillette today, and we were caught in this terrible storm. It does not look as though we can make it much farther tonight, but—"

"I understand," said the stranger. "Bring your family inside."

As he went back to the car, Gerald was thinking of the blessing it is to have a "shelter in the time of storm." Emily was waiting expectantly when he arrived at the snow-laden convertible. "We can stay here for the night, Emily. Give me the boy, and we will go inside to get warm."

The strangers were very friendly and cordial. The housewife hastened to prepare some hot soup for them to eat and a warm, comfortable bed where they might rest after the exhaustion of the night's drive.

Their host, Mr. Jones was telling Gerald something. Emily listened attentively as he recited the events of the evening. "You see, Mr. Ziska, two cars of tourists were caught out here earlier tonight, and they thought it best not to try to make the trip through the badlands in this blizzard. When they had parked their cars at the roadside, they came here and asked to use our telephone. Calling Sheridan, they succeeded in getting a truck to come out and take them all back into town.

"After they left, I looked out and noticed that the lights had been left on in both cars. Thinking that traffic had probably ceased until the road was cleared by a snowplow, I went outside to turn off the lights.

"With the first car's lights turned off, I went to the second. Mr. Ziska, I could not turn off those lights no matter how hard I tried. I pressed, pulled, and twisted every button on the dashboard. Would you come out with me? Maybe you can find where the light switch is."

The two men went out, and Mr. Jones, to his utter amazement, turned the lights out himself. He did it with absolutely no difficulty.

"Mr. Ziska, I do not understand it! Why did those lights refuse to go out before?"

"If it had not been for those lights," said Gerald, "we would never have seen the shadow of your house."

When the men returned to the house, Emily was telling Mrs. Jones about their praying for guidance and shelter. "The Lord kept those lights on for us in answer to our prayer," said Gerald. "He has performed a miracle to save our lives."

The Joneses were deeply impressed. Although it was late when Gerald and Emily said their prayers, it was with a deeper consecration and hearts filled with gratefulness to a heavenly Father who watches and cares for His own in times of distress. ❧

*T*his story, too, was originally published in The Youth's Instructor *during the 1950s. Judging by the number of angel stories to be carried by that magazine, spiritually based angel stories were deeply appreciated by their editors during the* 1930s, 1940s, 1950s, 1960s, and 1970s.

In Betty Jones's New Jersey story, we are not permitted to see the faces of the "angels" (that identity is strongly implied by circumstantial evidence). It always intrigues me to compare the numerous variations in how angels interface with us—there certainly is no norm or template.

Guardian Angels

Betty Jones

It was an extremely dangerous road for a mother and her two daughters to take. Brutal outlaws had taken virtual control of certain sections of it. But surely God's angels would protect them—but how?

Mrs. Jackson sat behind the wheel of her car, peering out at the deserted mountain road that lay ahead of her.

Through this remote, uninhabited territory she had driven for the past two hours, not once taking her eyes off the winding course that lay beyond.

She was not afraid, although others would have been, and they would have had reason to be, too. Before leaving her home, she and her two children had knelt down to ask their heavenly Father's guidance and protection on their journey. Mrs. Jackson made this a common practice, and the Lord had always seen fit to bring them safely to their destination.

This was the loneliest section in northern New Jersey. Along this country road lurked thieves and robbers waiting for the right moment to pounce upon their prey. Everyone had been warned to beware of these brutal outlaws.

Newspapers for miles around had carried stories of manslaughter and thievery. Those who must travel this road were warned by the authorities not to stop their cars for anything. It might result in the loss of their lives.

"Mommy, what was that?" questioned little Ellen excitedly.

Mrs. Jackson had been so absorbed in her own thoughts that she had not heard her daughter's question until it was repeated a second time. She had not seen anything. About what could Ellen be talking?

"But, Mommy, I'm sure I saw something. See, over there in the trees. It's moving around!" Her mother glanced in the direction in which Ellen was pointing. A look of sudden terror swept over her face and just as quickly changed into relief. It was nothing more than the reflection of the headlights in the trees beyond.

Yes, they had prayed, but still for some reason the children were very much afraid.

Their mother reminded them that the Lord protects His own, and nothing can happen to them unless it be in harmony with His will. These words proved to be very comforting, and in a short time all reflections of the previous minutes had vanished from their minds.

"Mother," questioned Ann, the younger of the two, "what makes people so mean and cruel that they want to steal and kill others just to get their money? If I were a thief and a robber, I'd do everything I could to make people happy. I would be nice to them, just like Jesus would have been."

Her mother smiled at her daughter's childlike conception of what these unscrupulous men were like. If only it were that easy for them to reform! They were nearly halfway through this dangerous territory, but the most perilous part still lay ahead of them.

To the small group in the car, everything suddenly seemed darker. The moon had disappeared behind a cloud, a haze seemed to enclose them, making it impossible to see farther than a few feet beyond the headlights. The curves were getting more dangerous, and the driver knew that if she should lose control of the automobile or be stopped along this stretch, the car could be easily sent over the side of one of these cliffs and into the river below.

If only there were a house somewhere along the way, or just a passing car!

The two girls sitting in the backseat were too restless for sleep. Although their mother's words had comforted them for a long time, their imaginations were active, and they were peering out the back window, straining their eyes for what might possibly be the headlights of an automobile. It would make them feel so much better just to know that someone was near them and could help them if any trouble should arise.

But no—for miles now they had ridden, not seeing any evidence of a living animal, much less a human being.

Why had they chosen this particular night to start their trip? Why had they taken this route? All this remained a mystery in their minds.

Could God have a purpose in bringing them over this deserted road without any human help available for miles around?

Mrs. Jackson, not lifting her eyes from the road, breathed a silent prayer: *If God would only be with us and watch over us as He has in times past.*

As she glanced up into the rearview mirror, it seemed that suddenly, out of nowhere, two lights almost blinded her. From where had they come? Ann and Ellen both had been straining their eyes to see some sign of a traveler but had been unsuccessful.

They were so happy as the car drew nearer, for at last they did not have to be afraid, because they were no longer alone.

The lights though! They were so very blinding. Mrs. Jackson reached up to change the position of the rearview mirror, to remove the glare that was reflecting in her eyes, but somehow she could not do it. *That would be foolish,* she thought to herself. *Why, by just looking up into the mirror I can be very much comforted.* So with that thought in mind, she quickly started a humorous conversation with the girls.

At this Ellen and Ann were calmed, and before long the three of them felt at ease.

The car had been following close behind for almost ten miles now, without passing or even making an attempt to pass. Apparently, the occupants were in no particular hurry, or maybe they, too, felt safer following another car.

The road that lay just ahead was very narrow, and at this particular spot, it led straight up the side of the mountain without any woods or curves or intervening rise of ground to observe a clear view.

Suddenly, without realizing what she was doing, Mrs. Jackson jerked the car over to the side of the road into a small driveway. She had no idea that any such drive was there. Many times she had driven over this mountainous road, but she did not remember ever seeing this particular one—not even once.

Why had she done it? What had made her pull over to the side of the road without giving some kind of signal to the car that was following so closely behind?

Within a split second, these thoughts ran through her mind. She sat there with her hands clasped, and without hesitating, she lifted them to roll down the window of her car.

"I'm sorry," she began, "but I don't know what made me do it. Please believe me. Will you accept my most humble apology?"

There was no response, so she again asked for the other driver's forgiveness, thinking he had not heard her the first time. Still there was no answer. Where could he be? What could he be doing? She quickly turned to look behind her. The other car was nowhere in sight. It had disappeared!

She felt as though the very hosts of heaven were surrounding them. She knew then that God had kept His promise and had protected His own. He had answered their prayers.

After continuing the remainder of their trip and safely reaching their destination, they related to their friends this thrilling and mysterious experience.

The following day, Mrs. Jackson was glancing through the evening's paper when she noticed an article describing the arrest of two vicious criminals. After reading it, she found that the arrest had taken place the previous night at that very dangerous section of the country where the car had been following so closely behind her.

She folded the newspaper slowly and reverently opened her well-worn Bible as her lips silently formed the words of the promise she sought: "The angel of the Lord encampeth round about them that fear him, and delivereth them." ❧

I wrote this story eight years ago for an Epiphany book proposal; but since that proposal has not yet been accepted by a publisher, this is the story's first appearance in print.

As I look back over my life, I can clearly see that, just as is true with other known angelic interventions, I have kept angels more than a little busy getting me out of tight spots; a number, such as this one, resulting from too much testosterone and not enough brains. I am deeply humbled that God's angels have spent so much time and effort keeping the most unworthy of His children alive down through the years.

Hanging On by the Fingers

Joseph Leininger Wheeler

Has your life ever hung by only a slender thread?
Have you ever reached the very limits of your strength?
Is it possible to go beyond the impossible?

It was a golden Saturday afternoon on California's Howell Mountain overlooking the Napa Valley. Spring had painted the world in vibrant colors, so I just *had* to leave the college dormitory and escape. Foolishly, I hiked off alone; even more foolishly, I told no one where I was going.

After some time, I descended into Pope Valley and decided to do some exploring of ravines and canyons that were unfamiliar to me. As hours passed and I stumbled on one breathtaking vista after another, even a sixty-foot waterfall none of my classmates had ever seen, I grew bolder and took more chances.

Deciding to climb one canyon wall, I zigzagged my way almost to the top. I was holding on to a stone outcropping when my feet slipped out from under me, dislodging my foothold in the process. It took a long time for that displaced rock to reach the canyon floor.

Initially, I took the experience lightly, figuring I could easily find another foothold to my right or to my left. To my growing horror, I discovered that there was no other foothold! And when I looked down, I froze in terror, for it was certain death if I should let go.

And that brought home another reality: *How long could I hold on to the stone outcropping before my fingers would lose their grip?* Not much longer, I was certain.

They say that when you know you are going to die, your entire life flashes before you. I vividly remember that my twenty years of life did just that. But I also thought about all the years ahead that I had assumed were all but guaranteed: *You mean I'll never find the girl of my dreams? I'll never marry and have children? I'll never have a career? I'll never travel the world? What will the folks think? I know what they—what everyone—will think:*

"Of all the stupid things to do: hiking off alone! And taking foolish chances to boot. Way out there far away from people; what if he'd been struck by a rattler? He'd never have made it back on his own."

Then I thought about God. Was God going to just let me die? My fingers felt as though they could not possibly hold on a second longer. I prayed despairingly, "Lord, don't let me die! Please! I've barely begun to live. I know I did a stupid thing—but won't You save my life anyhow?" Like the wrestling Jacob, I wept and begged.

More time passed. It was almost surreal: I just could not believe I was still holding on. Suddenly, at an angle some distance below, I spied a shallow ledge. It was my only chance. I prayed again, begging God to spare my life and enable me to reach that ledge.

Then I let go, lunging at an angle with every ounce of energy I had left—and I hit it dead center, grabbed an overhanging manzanita bush, and managed to hold on until I finally stopped shaking.

Eventually, the shadows of evening beginning to darken the canyon, I left the ledge and found a path down to the canyon floor. It was late that night before I reached the college campus.

Even later, as I lay in bed looking up at the ceiling, my mind still whirling, and thanking God all the while, my thoughts veered back to my fingers: *Why and how had I been able to hold on so long? Why hadn't my fingers lost their grip and let me fall? Even before I prayed, how had I done it?*

But then I remembered that not until I'd turned the matter—my struggle to go on living—over to God, recognizing that I was totally incapable of finding a way out on my own, did I lose the incapacitating panic that had shut my brain down, and with clear eyes scrutinize the canyon below for a possible alternative to just letting go and falling to my death. Even after all these years, I'm convinced, beyond a shadow of doubt, that an angel directed my eye to that one stone life raft (a mixed metaphor if there ever was one!) that might save my life.

That was, of course, only half of the miracle; the other half was my despairing flailing leap for that ledge far below. Even if I hit it, dead center, as I did, I could just as easily have broken my ankle or sprained it so badly I'd have lost control and likely maimed or incapacitated myself. What was it the psalmist promised in Psalm 91:12? "They shall bear thee up in their hands, lest thou dash thy foot against a stone [or in this case, ledge]." ❦

SECTION TWO

Thou shalt not be afraid for the terror by night,
nor for the arrow that flieth by day;
Nor for the pestilence that walketh in darkness;
nor for the destruction that wasteth at noonday.
Psalm 91:5, 6 (KJV)

*T*his story is from The Youth's Instructor, *published during the 1940s. Written by Mildred Wilson, it chronicles what it is like to live through a tornado. While an angel is not actually seen, a very strong presence gets through to Sister with the message she articulates:* Let's get out of this house right now!

As is true with the vast majority of angel stories, prayer is a factor in the providential intervention of angelic forces.

Through the Storm

Mildred Wilson

At first they didn't worry—just some more rain. But then the cow came in early, the dog whined to be let in, the sky darkened, and then storm fury like they'd never experienced before. What should they do?

The monotony of a long spell of damp, cold March weather was finally broken by the dawn of a glorious spring day. The sun from a cloudless sky and the verdure of the grass accentuated the yellow of the daffodils on the lawn.

Orthie and I rose in high spirits. There was much work to be done, and we were eager to be at it. We must wash the family laundry, clean the house, finish unpacking the boxes that had not been opened since we had moved in a few weeks before, and bake a cake for the young people's party that was to be held in the evening at our cousin's home. It was to be a full day.

After a hearty breakfast, Mother, Dad, and Annie Laurie, a cousin who lived in our home, hurried off to their work in the city, leaving Orthie (affectionately called Sis by the family), Grandmother, and me to our duties.

We really enjoyed pinning the snowy-white clothes on the lines and watching them flap back and forth in the gentle breeze. The washing was soon over, and we attacked the boxes of dishes and books. We completed this task, gave the house a thorough cleaning, and were then ready to relax awhile.

"Look! The cow is standing at the gate, waiting to be let in, and it is only three-thirty!" my sister exclaimed later in the afternoon. This was unusual, for our cow never came up until about five o'clock. Sis opened the gate to let her in. Somehow, not realizing why, we decided to put her in the yard beside the house instead of in the barn.

The clothes that we had laundered earlier in the day were dry now. As we started to bring them in, raindrops began to fall. We had to hurry to keep the clothes from getting wet again.

"Look what big drops of rain," I remarked to Orthie as the drops began to fall faster, "but I don't think it will rain much—probably just a light spring shower." Then glancing toward the west, we noticed an angry, black cloud that seemed to be boiling in its fury.

"Well, it's a good thing our clothes are dry. Look at that cloud. We are really going to have a downpour," Orthie replied to my optimism. She folded the pieces that did not require ironing, stacking them neatly while I put them away in their respective drawers. Just as we were finishing this task, Chubby, our collie, came to the front door and whined to be let inside. Instead of lying down for a nap as she always had done when she was fortunate enough to get into the house, she would not leave our side. She continued to whine. Every time the thunder crashed, she would cry out in fear, as if trying to make us understand that we were in danger.

"What's the matter, you big coward?" Sis queried, playfully patting the dog on the head.

The sky was now dark as night, except for the streaks of lightning. Suddenly, the rain began to come down in torrents. Sis had gone to the kitchen to mix the batter for the cake, Grandmother was cooking supper, and I was in the front bedroom, making preparations for the party. It was almost time for the rest of the family to come home. Then the fury of the storm caused the electricity to go off, and we were left in total darkness. I felt my way into the kitchen, where Sis and Grandmother had already rallied to the situation by lighting a candle and were doing the cooking by its dim rays. As the storm did not seem to be dampening their spirits any, I remained cheerful, too. We southerners often witness these severe electrical disturbances; therefore, it was no unusual occurrence to us. But suddenly the torrential downpour changed from rain to hail. It was not until that moment that we thought of our poor cow tied near the house.

"Oh! I must put her under shelter," Sis cried, but Grandmother and I convinced her of the foolishness of risking her life for a cow. The wind was getting stronger every moment. It was blowing so hard that the kitchen door would not stay closed. Grandmother and I were braced against it, trying to hold it, when she shouted, "Orthie, come and help hold this door, while I go and lock the one in my bedroom, so the wind won't blow it open." She had just returned to the kitchen when we heard a huge cupboard of canned goods blow over on the back porch. "Oh, girls, it's going to blow the house away! Dear God, save us!" Grandmother prayed.

No sooner had she uttered these words than all three of us landed in a heap in the corner of the kitchen, along with chairs, cooking utensils, dishes, food, and the glass from a big window. I don't remember much that happened in the next few seconds. I held my hands over my head as I lay there listening to the crash of timber and glass all around, and then I lost consciousness.

How long I lay there I do not know, but it was probably only a few moments. The sound of Grandmother's groans and Sis's crying, "Help me; help me get her to the bed. I'm afraid she's hurt," brought me back to my senses. As Grandmother was rather heavy, we had to drag her to the bed. In our fright, we did not wait to see whether she was really hurt. When we got into the bedroom, what confusion we beheld! We could see the wallpaper hanging in shreds from the walls. The furniture was piled in the middle of the room.

"Get on the bed quickly, so that if the walls fall in, the bedstead will protect us," Sister commanded. Just then, the little collie landed in a heap in the middle of the bed, as if understanding Sister's words. It did not take us long to discover that nobody was seriously injured. As we prayed, our thoughts turned to our loved ones. Where were they? Would we ever see them again? How we prayed that they might get to us safely and quickly. We lay there for a moment too frightened and exhausted to think what we should do next.

Then, suddenly, Sister exclaimed, *"Let's get out of this house right now!"* No one questioned or wondered why she should make such a suggestion, but we made preparations to carry out her orders, even though we had no idea where we were going. We decided to try the next-door neighbor's home first. Through the blinding rain, we could not see whether it was still there or not.

We were the proud owners of a beautiful white Persian kitten, but we had no idea where he was now. I remembered seeing him in the front bedroom earlier in the afternoon, and Sis went to get him. It would never have occurred to us to leave that house without our pets. As she went into the bedroom, superhuman strength must have helped her get the door open, for later the doors had to be taken from their hinges in order to get from one room to another. She found the little kitten curled up on the bed, a thoroughly frightened ball of fur. I carried the dog, and Sis the kitten. Grandmother put a quilt around her in an attempt to keep off a little of the rain. We must have been a pitiful but comical sight, tramping through water that was knee-deep, trying to find a place of safety.

It took us only a short time to reach the neighbor's home, and joy of joys, it was still there. I knocked on the door, but there was no immediate response. The horrible thought came to us then that there might not be anyone at home. We prayed as we continued knocking, and somehow, above the roar of the storm, the woman heard and answered. She took us in, gave us dry clothing, and put us to bed.

Daddy had left his work when the heavy rain started, and was on his way to pick up Mother and Annie Laurie before coming home. He was just passing a service station when hail began to fall. Fearful that his automobile would be seriously damaged, he drove into the station and stayed there until he could see to drive again.

When he left the station, he had no idea that there had been so severe a storm. The Almighty Protector kept him from realizing it, because if he had known there was a tornado raging, he would have gone right into it in his anxiety about the family. He went by the little schoolhouse where Annie Laurie taught the church school, and then continued on to get Mother.

Suddenly, they awoke to the fact that something serious had happened. They began to see trees uprooted, signs turned over, and finally, as they drove farther into the stricken area, they saw that home after home had been completely destroyed. Then they realized fully what had happened, and Daddy drove as fast as he could to get to Mother. He found her safe, even though the building was badly damaged. She hurriedly came to the car and told him that she had stood in the back doorway and watched the cloud come from the very direction in which we lived.

Few words passed between them as they made the grim drive home. Daddy tried to reassure Mother, but the nearer they came to our home, the worse the situation became, and finally it was impossible for him to reassure her because of the terrible fear that was gripping his heart as ambulance after ambulance sped by, carrying the injured into town. It was almost impossible for him to drive, for the highway was filled with electric wires, trees, and debris.

As we watched for our parents to come, an ambulance came to take us to the hospital, but we realized that the hospitals would be filled with those who were seriously injured. Since we were not, we declined to go. Then, too, we knew that when Mother and Daddy came, it would only add to their anxiety to find that we were in a hospital.

After what seemed hours, the folks arrived, and the neighbor called to them to tell them we were in her home. I had never before felt so happy as I was when I saw that Mother and Dad were safe. After a glad reunion, they went to view our home. When they approached the house, the first thing they noticed was the cow still tied beside it. All the outbuildings and a big catalpa tree had blown into the barn. This made us realize why we had been impressed to tie the cow in the yard instead of putting her in the barn. The house had been blown twelve feet from its foundations. They opened the back door, but the room was so filled with gas from disconnected heaters that they dared not enter. Surely an angel had whispered to Orthie that we must leave the house. Daddy went to the garage to get his wrench, but found only debris where the garage had been. He finally found the wrench and cut the gas off at an outside cutoff.

When the house was finally cleared of gas, so that it was safe for them to enter, what a scene of desolation they found! The kitchen floor was a conglomeration of furniture, glass, cooking utensils, and half-cooked food, including the dough from Sis's cake. In the living room the furniture was turned helter-skelter. There was glass all over the floor. In the middle of the room, the rug humped up, and, curious to see what could cause such a hump, they lifted the rug and found a huge tree stump protruding through the floor.

That night in our other grandmother's home, the family doctor found us with many cuts and bruises, and Sis was suffering from a fractured foot. When friends and relatives came to offer their assistance, we learned that several people had been killed within a half mile of our home. This made us realize more than ever that it was only the hand of God that had kept the house from crashing down on us. Earnest prayers of thanksgiving ascended to heaven, for truly, "He shall give His angels charge over thee, to keep thee in all thy ways." ❧

*L*ois M. Parker's story was carried by a Youth's Instructor *of the 1950s. In it, a Russian girl foolishly dares the bitter cold subzero temperature and snow of Russian winter rather than waiting for her father to come after her. As time passes, she hears wolves, and attempts to hurry. But by this time, the girl is so weak that had it not been for an angel, she would not have made it through to her destination. She never does see the rescuing angel clearly, but does feel a hand on her shoulder and a soft voice in her ear. When she turns, she sees no one, nor are there tracks in the snow.*

An Angel Walked

Lois M. Parker

Her feet were so cold! She knew she was freezing to death. If that didn't get her, the wolves would. She just couldn't take one more step!

Have you seen her feet?" The hushed voice of the nurse dropped lower. "I'll show you."

Nurses see many tragic things. This must be most unusual, I thought, to affect the girl in white in such a way. I followed.

A tiny wizened face turned to us from the white pillow. I did not notice the age lines or emaciation at first. Dominant as always were her eyes, alert and interested.

She had never been conspicuous in church. Only by accident had I noticed her earnestness in following the services, the radiance in the little aged face bowing in prayer or nodding an unspoken Amen. Her lips had formed the words of the hymns, and one felt that she joined an angel chorus in her mind, though she made no sound.

Now she could attend church no longer. Her labored steps could not carry her to the services she loved, so when she lay in the hospital, with few visitors, I felt that I must go to see her.

"Sophie, here is a visitor," the nurse cheerfully announced. "She is a nurse too. Do you mind if I show her your feet?"

Brightness bloomed in her face as she stretched a hand to me.

"Oh, my friend! It is so good of you to come. Yes, of course, Nurse, show her the old stubs. They are good for nothing now but to remind me that angels walk with men."

The feet. They were purple and swollen beyond much semblance of humanity. The darkened color served to make more distinct the white scars that marred toes, instep, ankle. The scars were very old, I could see, and I wondered what ordeal had brought them. It was a relief to have them covered again.

Sophie smiled.

"Put them away. No one would want to look at them long. They're no good now, but many and many the mile they have walked. Thirteen children I raised, and worked in the fields besides, so you see they have done their work. Let them rest."

As I held her shrunken hand, the question must have shown on my face.

"You would like to hear a story, ya?"

The forests of Russia, long ago, were thick and dark. Even in the little village, safely shut in by walls and lighted by candles, one could sometimes hear the wolves. It was good to be safe inside, with wood and food at hand.

No one risked the narrow forest roads at night, and even in daylight the men went out never less than two at a time. But the villagers were comfortable and safe—if they had shelter, wood, and food.

The people belonged to the land, and each family must serve their lord a certain time, to pay for the privilege of living.

At the castle, a long day's drive from the village home, Sophie looked anxiously out over the snowy fields. Still no dark speck coming out of the forest, to grow into her father's team and sled.

She was no longer needed, or even wanted, in the castle. Her term of three months' service had been broken by a trip home to care for a dreadfully ill mother, so she had stayed on at the castle two weeks later than the other village young folks.

It would have been such a merry ride home with them, she thought. Those now at the castle were strangers and uninterested in her, sometimes even mocking her village ways. She was eager to get home, and her father had promised to come for her.

With sudden decision, she whipped her babushka over her head and tied it firmly. Long since she had put on the felt boots and overboots. Now, as a "town" girl giggled and pointed at her rustic clothing, Sophie gathered her small bundle of belongings and started out, her determined little chin set.

At first the road was broken. Wood sleds had been out since the new snow. Her feet were as light as her heart as she thought of home and her family.

Long before the tracks ended, the castle was out of sight. The fields were fewer and the forests were closing in.

Before Sophie lay an unbroken trail, a winding white ribbon between dark walls of green. She hesitated, a little doubtful, then reassured herself aloud.

"Father promised he would come for me this morning, and surely, just around a bend or two, I will hear the bells of his sled."

She stepped briskly into the deep snow. It was light and fluffy, quite fresh, and it was not hard walking, even though it came well above the tops of the felt boots. The sun shone, and once in a while the harsh note of a winter bird assured her that the snow had not covered all life.

She was very strong in spite of her small size, and she delighted in the rhythmic swing of walking. It was an hour or more before the stillness of the woods began to oppress, and she slowed, a doubt stirring about the wisdom of going farther.

Snow had begun to work between the tops of the felt boots and her legs. The boots were old and not as snug as they should have been. There was a wet band around the thick woolen stockings where the snow had melted. She dug out some snow, but could feel the wetness going down inside.

Perhaps I should go back, but they don't need me, and there is hardly space for an extra in the girls' room.

As she stood thinking, a faint far sound vibrated through the forest. Not sure at first what it was, she turned to listen. Again the distant sound came, and she knew.

She could not go back. There were wolves behind her—far away, but between her and the castle.

She gasped a little but without wasting a moment went on, every step an emphasis to the prayer she whispered.

"Lord of heaven, be with me, help me!"

Walking was no longer fun. Her ears were straining, both for the jingle of bells and for the wolves. Sometimes she found herself running and breathless. Then, fighting panic, she walked again.

For long minutes there was silence except for her own breath and footsteps. Silence—perhaps even a half hour, until the moaning cry came again, always a little closer.

They aren't hunting in earnest or they would come faster, she thought desperately.

Her feet were all wet now inside the boots, and she was tiring. The sun commenced to slip down the western slope, toward early nightfall. There was a pain in her side. When she slowed, to attempt to ease it, the eerie call would again spur her on.

Her feet were so cold. If only she could rest—she was getting so tired. It was an effort to push her feet through the snow, and she could no longer lift them very high.

The trail behind her was erratic, for she could not walk steadily.

There was a low branch hanging over the road. She would go that far at least, before she stopped. Then when the branch was reached, she set another goal, farther on.

Like a refrain, her prayer went on and on. There was no strength to say it aloud. *Father, help me. I need Thee. Help me. Send an angel to help me. Lord of all, be with me*—over and over, with a little change of words, but always the cry, *Help, Lord!*

Her strength failed until she could barely reach a fallen stub. As she leaned against it, with sobbing breath, faintness almost overwhelmed her.

She felt a hand on her shoulder, and a soft kind voice spoke in her ear. *"You cannot rest now, Sophie. Go on."*

Stupid with weariness, she turned, but no one was there. Save hers, there was not even a track in the snow. In bewilderment, she pushed away from the stub, and from somewhere came renewed strength.

One step after another, one after another, while her mind forgot to listen for the wolves. Her prayer now was partly a plea and partly, faintly, questioning.

Lord, help me. Oh, Father, was it—who was it? No one was there! Oh, be with me, Lord. I know it must have been!

And a throbbing of her heart would send a surge of warmth to the cold hands and almost to her numbed feet. They were no longer cold, which was a relief, though somewhere in the fog of her brain, a warning note tried to get through.

She was tiring again, forgetting the wolves, everything but shoving first one foot then another through the snow.

The sun was down. In the growing darkness, the upward rise looked familiar. It *was* familiar. She had climbed it many times and rested for a while on the log bench at the top,

above the village. If only she could get that far.

It seemed an age before she stumbled into the snow-covered seat and fell upon it. Below, the village lights gleamed out on the whiteness.

It was too far. Sophie's head sank and she felt blackness creeping about her. A hand seized her shoulder and shook her into wakefulness.

"Sophie!" Again the clear, gentle voice was insistent. *"You cannot rest yet! Go home!"*

Against her will, she was raised to her feet and started down the road. Her rebellious legs could not tell when her feet touched the ground, and she stumbled again and again before falling against a door.

All at once, her father's face was above her, filled with consternation, lights about her, voices exclaiming, and arms bearing her into warmth that was almost unendurable.

Sophie put her hand out to me again.

"My father never forgave himself. He had good reason not to come, for my uncle had died and was buried that day. I should not have left the castle at all till he came, so it was not his fault."

She smiled a little, remembering.

"It was a year before I could stand on my

feet. They were frozen solid, and it is a miracle that I did not lose them both. My father would hold me and rock me, night after night, when I could not sleep for the pain.

"They were pretty good feet after a while. Oh, always they were sore, and hurt when it was cold, but I could use them. Now it is time for them to rest. And someday soon—"

The light in her face was pure glory.

"There were no tracks on the snow. Someday soon I will see the angel who walked with me!" ❧

*T*his 1924 Youth's Instructor *story was written by an unknown writer; we know only that he was a train engineer who experienced the miracle depicted in this story. The train and all within it are saved from probable death by a man who had been awakened much earlier than normal, and while seated at breakfast, a voice seemed to say to him,* Go to the railroad, *again and again, until he did so. Only when he reached the tracks did he discover why.*

It is typical of a number of angel stories in that while they don't actually hear the angel's voice, they might as well have as the insistent commands are such that it proves impossible to resist them.

The Telegram That Saved My Train

Author Unknown

The train engineer had a strange premonition that peaceful evening. Then the premonition left him. Hey! What was that man running down the tracks for? Did he want to get killed?

It was long past midnight when the long B & O train from Saint Louis, bound for Cincinnati and the East, pulled into Washington, Indiana. The train was heavily laden with passengers, for there had been a great gathering in Saint Louis, and hundreds of people were returning to their eastern homes. There were seven sleepers, one day coach, and one baggage and combination car.

Jim and I had been preparing for our night's run. Jim was the fireman and I the engineer, and it was our duty to take charge of this train at Washington and go on with it to Cincinnati. As we fired the engine that night, a strange burden seemed to weigh upon me. I could not account for it. I felt as if something was going to happen. I didn't know what. I told Jim how I was feeling. He and I were both Christian men, and we decided we had better pray before we left the "ready track," so

we knelt together and committed ourselves and our train to Him who sees in the darkness as well as in the light. Thus with lips and hearts still warm with prayer, we started on our night's run.

It was a beautiful night. Never did our train glide along more gracefully over the rails. Through the tunnels and around the curves she flew, and promptly on time we pulled into Seymour, Indiana. More than half the state of Indiana had been crossed, and the most dangerous part of our journey was past. It was almost morning now. My strange premonitions of the night had fallen from me, and I said to Jim, "I feel better now." With fear gone and a light heart, I put my hand to the throttle as we started out of Seymour.

When our train was about five miles east of Seymour, near Storm Creek Bridge, the first rays of dawn were just seen as I saw a man running down the track toward me, waving his hat frantically. I applied the emergency brake and brought my train to a standstill as quickly as I could. I noticed that he was very much excited and asked him what the trouble was. "A broken rail," he cried, "just ahead of your engine!" I got down from my engine and looked, and sure enough, there on the top of a deep fill I saw that a great piece of the rail was broken off and thrown out of its place.

"Well, thank God for answering prayer!" I said and then turned to the man who had flagged us. "What brought you out on the track at this early hour?" I asked.

Then he told me how he and his wife had been awakened at a much earlier hour than usual that morning, and while they were seated at the breakfast table, something seemed to say to him, *Go to the railroad; go to the railroad; go to the railroad!* and yet again the insistent call, *Go to the railroad!* He jumped up from the table and started out. His wife said, "Where are you going?"

"I am going to the railroad," he answered.

"What for?" she asked.

"I don't know," he said.

"Hadn't you better finish your breakfast before you go?" she urged. But he was gone.

Down across the field he went, over the rail fence, and stepped on the track. He cast his eyes along the track, and right before him,

on the top of the twenty-foot fill, he saw a broken rail. For a moment, he stood trying to think what he should do. From what direction would a train come first? He had not long to think, for just then his ear caught the distant rumble of the night express coming out of Seymour and—well, I knew the rest of the story.

"Are you a Christian?" he asked. I told him I was, and the next moment we were down on our knees on the ground together giving thanks to God for this deliverance.

While we were praying, my conductor came up to us and said, "What's the matter?"

"Look here," I said, pointing to the broken rail. "We are just thanking the Lord for sparing our lives and the lives of all the people on this train, including yours." We told him the whole story, and he, though a non-Christian, said it was a wonderful deliverance, and added fervently, "Thank God for the man who saved us!"

We repaired the broken rail well enough so that we could pass over it very slowly, and left our head brakeman to stop any other approaching train till the matter could be reported and properly attended to. We thanked the old farmer, bade him goodbye, wishing God's blessing on him and his wife, and on we sped for Cincinnati.

Arriving safely in the Grand Central depot in Cincinnati, I leaned up against the cylinder of my engine and watched the crowd from my train go by. Some were happy and said cheerily, "We are glad you got us in so nearly on time." Others passed by with their heads in the air; and none of them knew how near death's door they had been that morning, nor of the grateful prayers that had been offered at the front of the train just at dawn.

Two days later, I learned that the opposing train to mine—number fifty-five going west—had broken that rail as they passed over it, and had felt the jar of it severely. They had notified the train dispatcher at Seymour to warn me to look out for a broken rail just east of Storm Creek Bridge, but for some unexplainable reason, the message never reached me. Jim and I knew that it was the other message—the telegram sent us by way of heaven—that saved our train. ❧

*B*arbara Westphal's missionary stories mean more to me than to most since she and her husband served in the same Latin American mission field my folks did. In fact, my mother, also a Barbara, considered Barbara Westphal to be a cherished friend. Our family and the Westphals, while in Panama, spent a lot of time together.

Barbara Westphal wrote many missionary stories and books; this colporteuring story was published in The Junior Guide. In this account, the two rescuing angels appeared as angel policemen on horseback. At the conclusion of their providential intervention, the angelic police vanish.

Having sold Christian books door-to-door for five summers during my college years, I can just imagine the thoughts that swirled around in Emma's and Irene's heads. Just to think of all that hard-earned money for the entire summer snatched from them by a thief! And, by extension: realize they'd just lost an entire year of education.

WHEN ANGELS RODE HORSEBACK

Barbara Westphal

The man had been friendly all right. Too friendly, *Emma thought.*
Why did he ask so many questions about the money they were collecting?
But surely such a polite gentleman couldn't be a thief.
Could he?

I think we had better stay in this village tonight," Emma said to her friend. "I don't want to walk back to the other village through the dark with this precious briefcase."

She tugged at the heavy bag—heavy with pay for the books the girls had delivered, heavy with the *columbuses* (money) they had taken in that day.

"I'm not staying *here* tonight," declared Irene. "I want to sleep in my own bed."

Emma had begun to sell books for a scholarship when she was only fourteen. Now, after two years in an Adventist academy in Central America, she was an experienced colporteur.

"No, Irene," she said now, "it would be too dangerous to walk an hour in the dark by ourselves with all this money. If we had fin-

ished sooner, it would have been different; but our deliveries took us longer than we expected."

"Oh, you're always so cautious! I'm not one bit scared."

"Haven't you noticed that a man has been following us most of the day?" asked Emma.

"You mean that polite fellow who is so interested in our work? Oh, he's just being friendly."

The man had been friendly all right. *Too friendly,* Emma thought. He had asked if this were the day the girls were delivering books. The next time he met them, he inquired if the girls were having good success collecting the money. And the next time, he had even offered to accompany the girls back to the village where they had been staying. How did he happen to meet them so often? Emma wondered.

Well, maybe Irene was right. A polite, well-dressed gentleman, such as he was, surely couldn't be a thief.

No one likes to be a coward or to be laughed at, so Emma gave in before her friend's insistence, and the two girls started out of the village. It was obvious that darkness would close down on them in a few minutes, for it was already twilight, and that magic time lasts only a few minutes in the tropics.

There was a long stretch of straight road and then a sharp turn. As the girls rounded the first curve, where they could no longer be seen from the village, they saw a man on horseback—the same man who had been so interested in their welfare.

"Give me that bag!" he demanded.

"No, it's not heavy," Emma replied evenly, pretending not to know they were being held up.

"This is no joke," the man snarled. "GIVE ME THAT BAG!"

The girls knew they could not fight with him—and they saw a revolver in his belt. So they let him take the bag without resisting.

Emma still tried to be polite. "Sir, everyone in town knows you're an honorable man. I am sure you wouldn't take away from us what we have worked so hard to earn." Even as she spoke, she had a sick feeling inside, thinking of the loss of the six hundred columbuses that were to have paid for her and Irene to go back to school. How hard they had worked these last three months taking orders! She remembered the tired feet, the headaches, the hot sun, the missed meals. Was it all to be for nothing?

Suddenly, two handsome policemen appeared on horseback, well-armed.

"Are you girls selling books?" they asked courteously. "Are you in trouble?"

"Yes," they sighed with relief, for the thief was already dropping their bag on the ground, putting spurs to his horse, and rushing away.

Thankfully, Emma picked up the precious briefcase and looked around to thank the two mounted policemen. They were nowhere to be seen! Yet the girls had not heard the hoofbeats of their horses on the ground!

"Irene, did you ever see mounted police before in our country?"

"No. I surely never heard of policemen on horseback before, not around here, anyway."

Emma looked up and down the darkening road as she said reverently, "They weren't policemen. They were angels!" ❧

This is one of the longer stories recorded in W. A. Spicer's classic angel anthology, The Hand That Intervenes. *Spicer synthesized it from the autobiography penned by the famed missionary John G. Paton. It is different from most of the other angel stories in this collection in that, while the stories are episodic, each portion is a self-standing story—one long saga of incredible angelic interventions and miraculous preservation of Paton's life in the New Hebrides back in 1858.*

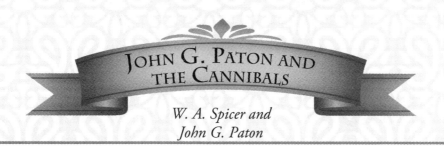

John G. Paton and the Cannibals

W. A. Spicer and
John G. Paton

Had these incredible accounts not been subsequently confirmed by the very cannibals who attempted to kill John G. Paton, one would wonder if Paton had been stretching the truth. One thing is sure: Had not Paton been a man of absolute faith in his God, he could not have endured the continual attacks they launched on him.

One of the classics of missionary literature is John G. Paton's story of his life in the New Hebrides, in the South Pacific Ocean. He first landed on the island of Tanna in the year 1858, as a missionary of the Reformed Presbyterian Church of Scotland. Again and again, Mr. Paton was surrounded by fierce cannibals, gathered with the determination to kill him and all those who were friendly to him.

Mr. Paton tells of many wild scenes and his wonderful deliverances. Of one occasion he wrote:

"Frenzy of excitement prevailed, and the blood-fiend seemed to override the whole assembly; when, under an impulse that surely came from the Lord of pity, one great warrior chief who had hitherto kept silent, rose, swung aloft a mighty club, and smashing it earthward, cried aloud: 'The man that kills Missi must first kill me; the men that kill the mission teachers must first kill me and my people; for we shall stand by them and defend them till death.'

"Instantaneously, another chief thundered in with the same declaration; and the great assembly broke up in dismay.

"All the more remarkable was this deliverance, as these two chiefs lived nearly four miles inland, and, as reputed disease makers and sacred men, were regarded as among our bitterest enemies."

Again, the missionary wrote:

"One day, while toiling away at my house, the war chief and his brother and a large party of armed men surrounded the plot where I was working. They all had muskets, besides their own native weapons. They watched me for some time in silence, and then every man leveled a musket straight at my head. Escape was impossible. Speech would only have increased my danger. My eyesight came and went for a few moments. I prayed to my Lord Jesus. . . . I tried to keep working on at my task, as if no one was near me. In that moment, as never before, the words came to me, 'Whatsoever ye shall ask in My name, I will do it;' and I knew I was safe.

"Retiring a little from their first position, no word having been spoken, they took up the same attitude somewhat farther off, and seemed to be urging one another to fire the first shot. But my dear Lord restrained them once again, and they withdrew."

A few days later, natives in large numbers were assembled about his house:

"A man furiously rushed on me with his ax; but a Kaserumini chief snatched a spade with which I had been working, and dexterously defended me from instant death.

"Life in such circumstances led me to cling very near to the Lord Jesus; I knew not, for one brief hour, when or how attack might be made; and yet, with my trembling hand clasped in the hand once nailed on Calvary, and now swaying the scepter of the universe, calmness and peace and resignation abode in my soul.

"Next day a wild chief followed me about for four hours with his loaded musket, and though often directed toward me, God restrained his hand. I spoke kindly to him, and attended to my work as if he had not been there, fully persuaded that my God had placed me there, and would protect me till my allotted task was finished. Looking up in unceasing prayer to our dear Lord Jesus, I left all in His hands, and felt immortal till my work was done.

"Trials and hair-breadth escapes strengthened my faith, and seemed only to nerve me for more to follow; and they did tread swiftly upon each other's heels. Without that abiding consciousness of the presence and power of my dear Lord and Savior, nothing else in all the world could have preserved me from losing my reason and perishing miserably. His words, 'Lo, I am with you alway, even unto the end of the world,' became to me so real that it would not have startled me to behold Him, as Stephen did, gazing down upon the scene."

Yet again:

"One evening I awoke three times to hear a chief and his men trying to force the door of my house. Though armed with muskets, they had some sense of doing wrong, and were wholesomely afraid of a little retriever dog which had often stood betwixt me and death. God restrained them again; and next morning the report went all round the harbor that those who tried to shoot me were 'smitten weak with fear,' and that shooting would not do."

Later on:

A powerfully built sacred man of the island, having publicly suffered defeat in an attempt to kill the missionary by sorcery, now determined to kill him with a warrior's spear. Paton says:

"For weeks thereafter, go where I would, he would suddenly appear on the path behind me, poising in his right hand that same Goliath spear. God alone kept it from being thrown, and I, using every lawful precaution, had all the same to attend to my work as if no enemy were there, leaving all other results in the hands of Jesus."

Still later, a savage aimed a blow at the missionary with a tomahawk. Paton avoided it, and said, "My Jehovah God is here to defend me now."

Trembling, the man looked fearfully about, and dared not follow farther. The fear of Jehovah again restrained the savage heart.

When in his old age, Missionary Paton was visiting his homeland, one little girl, in whose home he was to be a guest, asked her father, "Is it the real Dr. Paton who slid down the rock, that is coming to see us?"

"Yes, dear," said her father, "the very same."

"And, Papa," she asked with glowing eyes, "will his coat be dirty where he slid down the rock?"

She had heard the story of Paton's deliverance from savages that dark night on Tanna, when he slid down a precipice, asking God to save him from destruction. In his story of early days on Tanna, he gives the incident as follows:

"Having made half the journey, I came to a dangerous path, almost perpendicular, up a great rock round the base of which the sea roared up. With my heart lifted up to Jesus, I succeeded in climbing it, cautiously grasping roots and resting by bushes till I safely reached the top. There, to avoid a village, I had to keep crawling slowly along the bush near the sea, on the top of that great ledge of rock—a feat I could never have accomplished, even in daylight—but I felt that I was supported and guided in all that life-or-death journey by my dear Lord Jesus.

"I had to leave the shore and follow up the bank of a very deep ravine to a place wide enough for one to cross, and then through the bush away toward the shore again. By holding too much to the right, I missed the point where I had intended to reach it. Small fires were now visible through the bush; I heard the voices of the people talking in one of our most heathen villages.

"Quietly drawing back, I now knew where I was, and easily found my way toward the shore; but on reaching the great rock, I could not in the darkness find the path down again. I groped about till I was tired. I feared that I might stumble over and be killed; or, if I delayed till daylight, that the savages would kill me. I knew that one part of the rock was steep-sloping, with little growth or none thereon, and I searched about to find it, resolved to commend myself to Jesus and slide down thereby, that I might again reach the shore and escape with my life.

"Thinking I had found this spot, I tossed down several stones and listened for their splash, that I might judge whether it would be safe. But the distance was too far for me to hear or judge. At high tide the sea there was deep; but at low tide I could wade out of it and be safe. The darkness made it impossible for me to see anything. I let go my umbrella, shoving it down with considerable force, but neither did it send me back any news.

"Feeling sure, however, that this was the place I sought, and knowing that to await the daylight would be certain death, I prayed to my Lord Jesus for help and protection, and resolved to let myself go. First, I fastened all my clothes as tightly as I could, so as not to catch on anything; then I lay down at the top on my back, feet foremost, holding my head downward on my breast to keep it from striking on the rock; then, after one cry to my Savior, having let myself down as far as possible by a branch, I at last let go, throwing my arms forward and trying to keep my feet well up. A giddy swirl, as if flying through the air, took possession of me; a few moments seemed an age; I rushed quickly down, and felt no obstruction till my feet struck into the sea below.

"Adoring and praising my dear Lord Jesus, who had ordered it so, I regained my feet; it was low tide, and since I had received no injury, I recovered my umbrella, and wading through I found the shore path easier and lighter than the bush had been. The very darkness was my safety, preventing the natives from rambling about. I saw no person to speak to till I reached a village quite near to my own house, fifteen or twenty miles from where I had started.

"I here left the sea path, and promised some young men a gift of fishhooks to guide me the nearest way through the bush to my mission station, which they gladly and heartily did. I ran a narrow risk in approaching them; they thought me an enemy, and I arrested their muskets only by a loud cry: 'I am Missi! Don't shoot; my love to you, my friends!'

"Praising God for His preserving care, I

reached home, and had a long, refreshing sleep. The natives, on hearing next day how I had come all the way in the dark, exclaimed, 'Surely any of us would have been killed. Your Jehovah God alone thus protects you and brings you safely home.'

"With all my heart I said, 'Yes! and He will be your Protector and Helper too, if only you will obey and trust in Him.'

"Certainly that night put my faith to the test. Had it not been for the assurance that I was engaged in His service, and that in every path of duty He would carry me through or dispose of me therein for His glory, I could never have undertaken either journey. St. Paul's words are true today and forever: 'I can do all things through Christ which strengtheneth me.' "

The time came when the missionary had to flee from the island. War had broken out between the tribes. Paton had fled from his home to the village of a friendly chief, Nowar, but now the enemy was coming upon them. The missionary says:

"On reaching Nowar's village unobserved, we found the people terror-stricken, crying, rushing about in despair at such a host of armed savages approaching. I urged them to ply their axes, cut down trees, and blockade the path. For a little they wrought vigorously at this; but when, so far as eye could reach, they saw the shore covered with armed men rushing on toward their village, they were overwhelmed with fear, and throwing away their axes and weapons of war, they cast themselves headlong on the ground, and they knocked themselves against the trees as if to court death before it came. They cried, 'Missi, it's of no use! We will all be killed and eaten today! See what a host are coming against us.'

"Mothers snatched up little children and ran to hide in the bush. Others waded as far as they could into the sea with them, holding their heads above the water. The whole village collapsed in a condition of indescribable terror.

"Nowar, lame with his wounded knee, got a canoe turned upside down and sat upon it where he could see the whole approaching multitude. He said, 'Missi, sit down beside me, and pray to our Jehovah God, for if He does not send deliverance now, we are all dead men. They will kill us all on your account, and that quickly. Pray, and I will watch!'

"We prayed as one can only pray when in the jaws of death and on the brink of eternity. We felt that God was near and omnipotent to do what seemed best in His sight. When the savages were about three hundred yards off, at the foot of a hill leading up to the village,

Nowar touched my knee, saying, 'Missi, Jehovah is hearing! They are all standing still.'

"Had they come on, they would have met with no opposition, for the people were scattered in terror. On gazing shoreward and around the harbor as far as we could see was a dense host of warriors, but all were standing still, and apparently absolute silence prevailed.

"We saw a messenger, or herald, running along the approaching multitude, delivering some tidings as he passed, and then disappearing in the bush. To our amazement, the host began to turn, and slowly marched back in great silence, and entered the remote bush at the head of the harbor. Nowar and his people were in ecstasies, crying out, 'Jehovah has heard Missi's prayer! Jehovah has protected us and turned them away back.' "

Again, later on . . .

Mr. Paton and Mr. and Mrs. Mathieson, two other missionaries on the island, were awakened one night on the island of Tanna, in the South Seas, to find the church next to their dwelling house in flames. The crisis had come. After many a deliverance, it seemed this time they were to be slain. Armed savages were all about. Mr. Paton ran out to tear down the reed fence by which the flames were being carried swiftly toward the mission house. A shout was raised, "Kill him! Kill him!"

Mr. Paton told them, " 'Dare to strike me, and my Jehovah God will punish you! He protects us, and will punish you for burning His church, for hatred to His worship and people, and for all your bad conduct. We love you all; and for doing you good only you want to kill us. But our God is here now to protect us and to punish you.'

"They yelled in rage and urged each other to strike the first blow, but the Invisible One restrained them. I stood invulnerable beneath His invisible shield and succeeded in rolling back the tide of flame from our dwelling house.

"At this dread moment occurred an incident which my readers may explain as they like, but which I trace directly to the interposition of my God.

"A rushing and roaring sound came from the south, like the noise of a mighty engine or of muttering thunder. Every head was instinctively turned in that direction, and they knew, from previous hard experience, that it was one of their awful tornados of wind and rain.

"Now note this: the wind bore the flames *away* from our dwelling place; had it come in the opposite direction, no power on earth could have saved us! It made the work of destroying the church only that of a few minutes; but it brought with it a heavy and murky cloud, which poured out a perfect torrent of tropical rain. Now note again: the flames of the burning church were thereby cut off from reaching the reeds and the bush; and, besides, it had become almost impossible now to set fire to our dwelling house. The stars in their courses were fighting against Sisera!

"The mighty roaring of the wind, the black cloud pouring down unceasing torrents, and the whole experience, awed those savages into silence. Some began to withdraw from the scene, all lowered their weapons of war, and several, terror-struck, exclaimed, 'That is Jehovah's rain! Truly their Jehovah God is fighting for them and helping them. Let us away!'

"A panic seized upon them; they threw away their remaining torches; in a few moments they had all disappeared in the bush; and I was left alone, praising God for His marvelous works. 'O taste and see that God is good! blessed is the man that trusteth in Him!' "

Next morning their enemies were jubilant, however, for it had been finally decided to kill the missionaries without further hesitation, and burn the house. Friendly natives crept in, weeping and terror-stricken.

Just then a cry was raised on the beach, "Sail O!" All eyes turned, and there, sailing into the bay, was the trading ship, *Blue Bell*. It was time to heed Christ's instruction: when persecuted in one place to flee into another, and here was the providential provision of the way. It was time to flee from furious Tanna. The missionaries got on board the *Blue Bell*, thanking God again for deliverance, timed to the very moment of their extremity.

In the years after, John G. Paton saw all Tanna transformed from savagery by the power of the gospel. ❧

*F*rances Daisy Duffie and Martha Duffie's story of the missionary doctor David Duffie tells the harrowing story of his bout with the dreaded, and usually fatal, bubonic plague—and it was, at least back when the story was written, endemic in Peru. When it appeared the doctor was sinking into the predicted fatal coma, he was saved by "angel hands."

THE TOUCH OF ANGEL HANDS

Frances Daisy Duffie
and Martha Duffie

Bubonic plague—a virtual death sentence for her doctor husband!
What would the young wife do?

David Duffie, his high fever in its second day, had just asked Daisy to get down the big medical book and look up the subject bubonic plague.

Daisy looked at her young doctor husband in terror. "*Bubonic plague!* You don't think it's bubonic plague, do you, David?"

She read aloud from the book, her voice trembling: "Bubonic plague may be carried by infected rodents. . . . Incubation period, one to six days. . . . Onset of illness is sudden, usually accompanied by high fever. . . . The first swelling appears on lymph node nearest site of inoculation. . . . Generalized swelling throughout lymphatic system follows. . . . Disease is endemic to Lake Titicaca area—"

Everything fitted. On Monday David had finally arranged to remove his medical books from the rat-infested warehouse in Puno where they had been stored. Friday afternoon

a slight swelling under his left arm. That evening a temperature of 104 degrees. *Just a bad case of flu,* he thought. Saturday night, the swelling now general, he first noticed the tiny telltale scratch on his hand and remembered the rat-infested warehouse. That's when he became suspicious.

Daisy read on silently, through stinging tears: "A crisis to be reached fifth or sixth day after onset of illness. . . . Can expect either improvement or turn for the worse. . . . Little hope after patient is in coma stage. . . . Coma deepens until death." She knew that bubonic plague was usually fatal. But then, as she read on, there was a little hope: "Sulfadiazine in large doses sometimes helpful. . . . Antibubonic serum, if given early in the course of the disease."

Of course! Antibubonic serum! She fairly leaped to her feet. She would start the sulfa immediately. She would cable Lima for the serum. Dr. Potts would come from Lima. Everything would be all right!

The cablegram was sent. It read, "Dr. Duffie, Bubonic plague. Send antibubonic serum. Urgent. Please reply."

Then she waited. Waited for the serum. Waited for the fever to drop. Waited for Dr. Potts to come. Waited for everything. Sunday passed, and Monday. Tuesday morning and still no word. In the meantime, she did everything she could. But nothing brought down the fever or relieved the pain.

On Tuesday afternoon, however, there seemed to be a change. David was quieter and in less pain. He could even sleep some. It seemed the crisis had passed. Daisy was relieved—until she realized what it all meant. The change was not for the better at all. David was beginning to slip into a coma!

Now she sent a second cablegram, this time paying extra so that it would be delivered to Dr. Potts's home and signed for. (Later she would learn that the first cablegram was never received at all. The second was promptly delivered to his home and signed for at the door by the maid. Dr. Potts was not at home, and the maid put the urgent cablegram in a top dresser drawer where the doctor found it two days later.)

Wednesday morning, David could not take food or swallow. It was difficult to arouse

him. Soon he was completely unconscious.

At 2:00 P.M., the clinic personnel gathered for special prayer for their doctor. And then Noel, the Argentine nurse, started out in his little Ford for the secondary school seven kilometers away. He would bring back a group of ministers and teachers for a special service of prayer and anointing.

Daisy, at two o'clock, was sitting at David's bedside. She could scarcely discern his breathing, and she noticed that fluid was beginning to form on his lungs. The words of the twenty-third psalm flashed into her mind: "Though I walk through the valley of the shadow of death, I will fear no evil: for thou art with me." But in her despair, she couldn't help asking silently, "Is God with me in this hour? Does He hear? Why, oh, why has He not sent help?"

At that moment, there was a knock at the door. It was Marcilino with word of an emergency at the clinic. A patient was hemorrhaging, and Noel was gone. Could she please come?

She told Marcilino to sit by the bed with his hand on David's pulse and let her know instantly if there was any change. She hurried out. The emergency was serious and took longer than she had expected.

Forty-five minutes later, she rushed back into the house. Marcilino was sitting on the sofa in the living room, nonchalantly leafing through a *National Geographic* magazine. She was indignant, and she was terrified. Both at once. Why had the usually dependable Marcilino disobeyed her instructions? Why was he in the living room? Had the terrible moment come while she was gone?

The boy was utterly mystified at her outbreak. Hesitatingly, he tried to explain why he had deserted the doctor. "The doctor told me to go out," he said simply.

The doctor told you? She choked now. "The doctor hasn't spoken for two days!" She couldn't say another word. Tremblingly, she pushed open the closed door, terrified at the thought of what she would find.

The bed was empty. In front of the dresser stood David, fully dressed, his stethoscope in hand!

"David Duffie, what are you doing?" she gasped.

"Oh, thought I'd better go over to the clinic and make rounds," he said pleasantly. "Haven't seen patients for several days, have I? What day is it, anyway?"

When the troubled little group of teachers arrived at three o'clock for the special prayer and anointing service, they were ushered into the clinic consultation room for a time of special thanksgiving. Dr. Duffie sat at the desk.

A look at Marcilino's careful notes revealed this: "2:20, doctor turned over in bed. 2:25, he asked me what I wanted and told me I could go."

It was at 2:20 that Noel had reached the school with the sad news. The men had dropped immediately to their knees!

Where is the angel in this remarkable story of healing? In the case of David and Daisy Duffie, all human help had failed. Cablegrams had been no help. The medicine had not come. The doctor from Lima had not come. But the unconscious doctor and his despairing wife were not alone. They were not without help. The touch of angel hands, directed by the Great Healer, had restored David instantly to health. ⁂

*S*tories come at me in so many forms: computerized, photocopied, typewritten, mimeographed, spirit-duplicated, handwritten, as well as in books, magazines, and so on. Many of these were mailed to me down through the years. This particular World War I story was written by Lt. Frank Lee, a British naval officer. My copy is a relic of that vanished technology called spirit-duplicating (impossible not to get purple all over you if you were handling fresh copies).

The story has to do with a very definite heard voice that commanded the officer to go forward—just in time, it turns out.

*Ships were being sunk all around them, both by torpedoes and by mines.
So what was that inner voice that told the young lieutenant to stop the ship? If he did so, his navy
career would probably be over.*

I finished my supper early and went up the ladder to the deck of one of His Majesty's submarine chasers. We were at a dock at Valetta, Malta, having come in from patrol for a much needed refit. We had been sent to the Mediterranean by the Admiralty as an answer to Germany's bid to end the war by a wholesale destruction of shipping. How nearly that bid came to success can only be told by statistics. At one time in that fateful year of 1918, England was only two months from starvation.

The dock was deserted, except for one man on watch, for half the crew were on shore leave. As I strolled along the deck, I put my hand in my jacket pocket, and it came in contact with a letter I had received on the last mail from my mother back in Canada. I drew it out and read again, "My son, I want you to promise me that you will read the 91st Psalm every day, and especially that part, 'Thou shalt not be afraid for the terror by night; nor for the arrow that flieth by day.' And also where it says, 'He shall give his angels charge over thee, to keep thee in all thy ways.' And remember, son, I am praying for you continually, and I know that His promises will be kept."

Thoughtfully, I put the letter back in my pocket. As I passed the engine room hatch, Perkins, the Scotch chief engineer, appeared.

"How are the engines, Perkins?" I asked him.

"I've been working on the starboard engine, Sir," he said. "There's another good day's work on her before she'll be right. She'll run now, but I'd hate to go to sea with her tonight."

"What about the port engine?" I said.

"Not so bad, Sir. But I'm getting the second

started on it tomorrow—if he's back from shore leave by then," he ended with a grin.

I went down the war-room hatch to my cabin, pushed aside a uniform discarded by my sub-lieutenant who was at the Union Club ashore, and sat down. I took out my mother's letter and reached for my Bible over my bunk. Turning to the ninety-first psalm, I read it slowly and thoughtfully, pondering that passage, "Thou shalt not be afraid for the terror by night . . ." Instinctively, I thought of those grim floating mines with their sensitive protruding fingers, and those sleek, deadly torpedoes that struck in the darkness without warning. Those were the menaces faced by the sub chasers every minute of their patrol. I read on, "For he shall give his angels charge over thee." His angels! His angels . . . and a mother's prayers. These "would keep me in all my ways." I did not know then how soon they would be put to the test.

Suddenly, my meditation was broken by a commotion on deck, and someone scrambled hastily down the ward-room ladder. Then a sharp knock at my door.

"Come in!"

One of my men stepped inside and handed me a signal from the commander. I tore it open and read, "Prepare to proceed to sea at once. I shall go with you. —Ballard."

Go to sea with one dependable engine and half a crew! It must be an emergency to bring such an order.

"Tell the cox and Perkins to make ready to go to sea immediately!" I told the man. He saluted and disappeared.

I went on deck where I met the chief rushing down from his interrupted supper, wiping the back of his hand across his mouth. He said, "Give me as much time as you can, Sir, on that starboard engine. Maybe we can manage with the port one until we get out of the harbor."

The coxswain was already forward assigning men to their stations. The commander came over the side. The men snapped to attention. As I saluted, I noticed the strained look on his weathered face. He said, "Another troopship sunk. Don't know whether it was a mine or a torpedo. Get there as fast as you can. I'll give you your course. You were the only ship in." And as he clipped out the words, he turned toward the chart house.

"I'll get under way, Sir, and get the course when you're ready," I told him, and he nodded.

In the wheelhouse, I rang down both telegraphs twice to the engine room to stand by. The port telegraph rang back to tell me that Perkins was ready with that engine.

"Cast off forward," I shouted.

"All clear for'ard, Sir."

"Let go aft!" I called, and rang down slow ahead on the port engine.

"All clear aft," came the reply from the cook, who in the emergency had been pressed into deck service.

"Hard a starboard," I ordered as the port engine answered and we swung out from the dock in a wide circle with one engine and half a crew.

I picked up the speaking tube and called Perkins in the engine room: "How is it, chief? Is your starboard engine ready yet?"

"Give me another five minutes, Sir," he begged.

As I hung up the tube, the commander poked his head in the door and asked if we couldn't give her a little more speed. I temporized, saying, "As soon as we're out of the harbor, Sir, we'll open up."

Spray was coming over now. The coxswain remarked that we were in for some weather. A sailor was closing all ports and battening down hatches. Another man was aft inspecting and setting the depth charges. The gunner had taken the tarp off the seven-pounder forward and was adjusting the sights and oiling the gun.

As we slid past the fort on shore, a sentry came smartly to attention. Just as we reached the end of the breakwater, the chief, who had been working desperately, rang up on the starboard telegraph. With a sigh of relief, I rang down slow ahead. The starboard engine sputtered, hesitated, then caught with a roar, and we pushed out into the Mediterranean to meet—we knew not what.

When we were clear of the harbor a few minutes, the commander, his binoculars glued to his eyes, pointed on our starboard bow to two Admiralty trawlers fitted for minesweeping and said, "Run down and pick them up and tell them to follow us."

The cox put the helm over and I ran down full speed on the port engine to bring her around. It did not answer immediately. Then I realized the second engineer would not be at his engine. The chief had both stations to fill, his own starboard engine and the port one as well. I prayed silently that we would not find ourselves in a position that night where a split second to carry out an order might mean destruction. The engine replied and something like a voice seemed to say to me, *"He will give His angels charge over thee."*

We were fast approaching the trawlers, so I wrote on a signal pad, "Ship sunk. Follow us full speed to rescue.—Ballard," and told the signalman to semaphore the order to the trawlers. A few moments later, he was on the forward deck, braced against the heave of the ship as he furiously wigwagged the message.

Then I heard the commander's voice once more as he said, "Give her everything she has." I hesitated for an instant, thinking of that already straining starboard engine. Then seizing both telegraphs, I rang down full speed ahead. It was a desperate appeal for a few more revs.

The commander had gone on deck again and, steadying himself against a stanchion, was gazing through his binoculars. We were running smoothly and the only sound was the throb of the engines and an occasional vicious slap from a wave as it hit the side and spilled over the deck. I glanced at the cox. His jaw was set. His gnarled hands gripped the wheel as he calmly and skillfully jockeyed that racing little ship through the breaking seas.

I looked astern. The trawlers had come up, and with black smoke belching from their funnels were pressing after us. The cook was standing aft at the white ensign, ready to lower it as soon as the red disc of the sun dipped below the horizon. My gaze snapped forward again to the lookouts, one on either bow, a double precaution for this dangerous run. They were staring directly ahead into the blinding sun.

The commander pointed ahead. Through my own binoculars, I could plainly see dark objects on the water. Small boats and rafts! All that remained of the grim tragedy. I lowered my binoculars again lest my eyes might be momentarily blinded by the glare of the low-lying sun and the whipping spray. Again my mother's words came to me, for some reason: *"Remember, son, I am praying for you con-*

tinually." Back there in Canada, it would be her bedtime. She was praying for me . . . *now*! I was glad of that.

Suddenly, something told me to go forward without delay. The urge was as distinct and imperative as though the commander had spoken and I did not question it, though I realized it had not been a human voice. Quickly, I hurried to the bow. What I saw chilled my blood.

Directly in our path was a floating mine, its curved surface just breaking the water. We were rushing on it with reckless speed. In a matter of seconds, our bow would crash into those detonating fingers and we would be blown into eternity with only a drifting oil slick to mark our grave.

I wheeled, took a single step and stopped. I knew I never could make the wheelhouse. Cupping my hands into a megaphone, I shouted, "Hard-a-starboard! Full speed astern!"

Would the coxswain understand? Could the chief, working alone, reach both engines in time? Would that patched starboard engine catch?

Only God knew the answer.

I saw the cox give the wheel a superhuman twist. Both telegraphs clanged together. The ship lurched to starboard. Over my shoulder I saw that barrel-shaped menace, its black prongs of destruction now discernible, almost beneath our bows. I closed my eyes.

Then the engines went into reverse, first the starboard and an instant later the port. The ship shuddered from stem to stern and writhed as if in deadly pain. As the engines took hold, she seemed to shake herself in that churning sea, reeling and floundering like a stricken horse.

I was thrown to the deck and my head crashed against a stanchion around which I managed to get my arm before blackness wiped everything out. But there was no explosion!

A sailor helped me to my feet as my head cleared. Still dazed, I looked over the side. There it was only a few feet away bobbing harmlessly on the sea. I shuddered, and then marveled as there came again to my mind that passage, *"He shall give his angels charge over thee."*

We backed up a bit and gave the gunner his chance. The first shot did it, and the ugly mine sank beneath the waves. The trawlers came up and we got under way. Soon we were among the boats and rafts of the survivors. There was still enough light to pick them up. Then we headed for the harbor.

As we neared home, running at half-speed without lights, the commander came into the wheelhouse. He studied me for a moment and then said quietly, "Well, my boy, what made you do it? Go for'ard, I mean. That's all that saved us. The lookouts were blinded by the glare."

I hesitated before replying. My thoughts turned back to the letter I had been reading when his orders sent us to sea. I saw my mother again, praying for me. I knew it was her prayers which had saved us. I recalled the scripture she had urged me to read, *"Thou shalt not be afraid for the terror by night . . . He shall give his angels charge over thee to keep thee . . ."*

The commander was still waiting. I said, "I'm afraid I didn't have much to do about it, Sir. Let's just say it was a mother's prayers . . . and His angels who must have had charge over us . . . to keep us." ❧

SECTION THREE

The Lord says, "I will rescue those who love me.
I will protect those who trust in my name."
Psalm 91:14 (NLT)

I grew up on this story, hearing it retold many times during my childhood and adolescence. I don't believe it is mere coincidence that my grandfather's sister—who heard the story over and over, firsthand at her father's knee—agreed to write it out for me by hand and then faxed it to me. I also referred to another account written by one of my cousins (Dorothy Johnson Muir's "Faith," published in the August 2, 1938, Youth's Instructor). Essentially, what follows is Lois Wheeler Berry's story, with Dorothy Muir's account and my own memories intertwined, on occasion.

It was bitter cold that night on the summit in the Sierra Nevadas. So cold they'd have to get back in the wagon and keep moving.
Little did they know what was ahead of them . . .

If ever a man had absolute faith in his God, it was my father. And God honored that faith many, many times. But while many miraculous happenings were tied to his medical ministry, there was one story that took place even before medical school—before I was born, in fact (one reason I've always envied my three older siblings). During my growing-up years, no story did we children request more often than this one, and Father never tired of telling it.

During the early 1890s, Father, for a time, sold Christian books. This particular story took place during the summer of '92; Father had been taking book orders in the then rather wild Shasta and Modoc Counties of northeastern California. So spectacularly beautiful was the scenery that Father determined to bring Mother along in the fall when he delivered the books.

So it was that, after camp meeting in Stockton, Father hitched his two horses to the wagon (already heavily loaded with books and supplies, for there were then mighty few places to stop for food), signaled Mother and the three children to board the wagon, slapped the reins on the horses' rumps, and they were off. Vacations were rare in those days; consequently, to the children this camping trip was incredibly exciting.

There were several book deliveries made in the Redding and Mount Shasta area (Mount Shasta, at 14,161 feet in elevation, dominates the skyline of that part of the state). Always there is snow on it, but in those days there was a lot more snow than we see today. After making those deliveries, they headed up the steep road toward the eastern side of the Sierra Nevada. The weight of all those books, five people, food, and camping quilts guaranteed a slow trip, but the children didn't care, for that meant more nights camping out under the stars.

Finally, as they approached the highest summit on the route, Father joyfully remembered that there was an inn there—fittingly called "Paradise Inn." How wonderful to sleep in a real bed for one night!

Alas! When they arrived about sundown, there were only smoldering ruins, a stark fireplace alone still standing, legacy of a swift-moving forest fire.

Father managed to find a place to camp under some trees which had somehow survived the fire, Mother fixed supper, and everyone else set up camp. After supper, at worship, Father asked the Lord to send His angels to protect them during the night.

The cold at that elevation was bone chilling—winter was in the air. Finally, Father and Mother held a family council: *What should they do?* Father remembered that there was a house about six miles farther, on the other side of the mountain; if they kept going, surely they'd be offered hospitality. The children, teeth chattering and unable to get warm, were easy to persuade. So all the bedding was loaded back in the wagon; the weary horses were rounded up and rehitched to the wagon. Before slapping the reins, Father once again prayed that the Lord's angels would protect them during the long descent.

Night fell quickly, and it was so dark they could almost feel it. Not being able to see the road, Father loosened the reins, tied them to the whipstock, and left it up to the horses to find their way down. It was at this part of the story that Father's voice always slowed as he struggled for emotional control. You see, horse-drawn wagon travel was incredibly noisy: the horses' every move, every step, every snort, every shake of the reins, could be clearly heard; same with the wagon: the great solid rims were never quiet as they battled through dirt, gravel, and rocks, the wind whipped at the canvas, and the wooden chassis with its leather supports continually creaked and groaned. It was for this reason that none of the five ever forgot that night. Not only could they not see because of pitch-blackness—*they could not hear*! The wagon did not squeak; the wheels could not be heard as they turned, nor could the horses' hooves—it was eerily silent! They only sensed that they were moving.

Occasionally, they would feel a jolt, and twice the wagon came to a complete stop. In each case, Father slowly got out and groped his way towards where the horses' heads were, and then stooped down to see what the problem was. In each case, he encountered logs, logs which he was able—somehow—to move. Then he groped his way back to the horses, then back to the wagon, reboarded it, and signaled the horses that the way was clear. Once again, there was absolute silence.

Not too long after the second stop, everyone experienced a hard jolt. Immediately, the jogging of the horses could be heard again, the wagon wheels could be heard again, and all the multitudinous wagon squeaks could be heard again.

After what seemed an entire night (but in reality, only about four hours), they saw, off in the distance—faintly at first—a light in a window. As they drew nearer, dogs began to bark; and then a man came out, with a lantern in his hand, curious as to who these unexpected visitors might be and where they might have come from. Father politely introduced himself and then explained how they had planned to stay at Paradise Inn, but finding only ruins there, they had just kept going, hoping that they could make it down the mountain safely, and trusting that they would be welcome to stay overnight at this rancher's house.

The rancher didn't believe him at all, and retorted, "Now, really, no joking, where did you come from?"

Father again reaffirmed his story.

The rancher exploded, "Why, man, you're crazy! No one has made it through in over five days. It is impossible! Just today a man tried to go through on horseback, but he could not! [And thus, preposterous to imagine that a *wagon* could get through!] A terrible forest fire has burned everything—trees, brush, and houses."

But Father stuck to his story. Once again, he asked if they could stay overnight, and if there was feed and shelter for the horses. "Of course," answered the rancher. After the children were put to bed, Father went out to unhitch and tend to the horses' needs, only to find out that the kind rancher had already taken care of them. Before retiring, Father and Mother knelt down and offered a prayer of thanksgiving.

The following morning, again the rancher asked Father for the truth, once again the answer was the same. The rancher then showed Father the road and the terrain over which he would have had to travel through. As Father's gaze took in that impassable vista of fallen trees and smoldering logs, he finally understood the rancher's disbelief. So Father explained to him how they had prayed for angelic protection before leaving the pass.

The last thing the family saw as they left the ranch was their host, with a gun on his shoulder, retracing their route of the night before, walking between their wagon-wheel tracks toward the spot where the wheel tracks stopped. ❧

*D*eloris Bigler's story, a Youth's Instructor *story from the 1950s, has to do with a terrific storm that blew up out of nowhere on Lake Huron. This particular story belongs to another angel story genre: a superhuman angelic force that is used when human force alone is incapable of accomplishing a task.*

THE HAND ON THE WHEEL

Deloris Bigler

"How's our little goody-boy tonight?" John Bruning made life mighty tough for Ray Brown, a professed Christian on board the Calcite.
Suddenly, the loudspeaker blared, "Attention, all hands! Storm approaching west-north-west."
Would any of them get out alive?

The night watchman waved our car on. "OK, ma'am, go right in!" he called, as we drove through the gate and entered a city of giants. Huge piles of limestone, like the symmetrical hills in a child's drawing, caught the headlights as we threaded our way along the valley drive among these man-made mountains.

Giant derricks and cranes formed grotesque skeletons against the overcast sky. Distant thunder rolled, and as our car came round a bend in the narrow drive, the lights touched the lake for a second, giving us a glimpse of the rough water. Foreboding of a storm filled us; the dark night was suddenly filled with fear for our loved one out on the lake.

We pulled up near the loading dock. There, aboard two lake streamers, sailors scuttled back and forth with a grace and deftness in their work found only in those who have learned the rhythm of a wave. Floodlights from above the loading chutes combined with the ships' lights to make the pier as bright as noonday. Crushed stone rumbled down the chutes into the holes of the ships with the force and sound of a distant earthquake. Shouting voices, off-key singing, and cheerful whistling gave the place the air of a noisy, open marketplace.

Aunt Marian slipped out of the driver's seat. "Stay in the car, children. I'll be right back." She slammed the door and hurried toward the company office, her head pressed against the strong June breeze.

Uncle Ray worked for a large limestone quarry in Michigan on Lake Huron. He was the oiler on one of the company's ships, the

Calcite, which was due to dock that night at eleven o'clock.

Aunt Marian came out of the company office, her brow furrowed in a little frown she wore when she was worried.

Joyce opened the car door for her mother. "What about Dad's ship, Mom?"

"Mr. Johnson says that a message just came through from the *Calcite;* they're in a bad storm, and they're running for cover behind an island." Aunt Marian's face showed signs of strain. "I think we'd better pray right now for the safety of the *Calcite.*"

Each one of us bowed his head and offered an earnest petition to God to watch over Uncle Ray and the ship.

Glancing up from his work, Ray Brown watched the majestic sunset on Lake Huron. Piles of thunderheads made a border of purple along the horizon, and a few clouds floated loose, like feathers escaping the ticking on pillow-making day. The water was choppy. Over it blew a cool breeze, refreshing after a day under the hot June sun.

"Looks like a storm tonight, eh, Brown?" queried one of his mates.

"Yes, Henderson, but I was thinking more about God's handiwork than storm warnings as I looked at the sunset."

Henderson raised his eyebrows and turned to his work. *That Brown, he sure does harp on religion all the time,* ran through his mind.

To his shipmates, Ray Brown seemed odd. Having lived all their lives in a community where religion consisted entirely of a worshipful attitude in church every Sunday, these men could not understand a man who brought his religion out of the church and into his daily life. They reacted like chickens when a new bird is added to their flock, pecking at first, but later just ignoring him.

With a sigh, Ray turned to his work. Would the men ever understand how real God is and how His hand guides and cares for them even when they do not serve Him?

Night settled over the *Calcite,* stifling the cool breeze, making the air oppressive, breathless. All sounds were intensified; voices bounced back and forth across the ship. As smoke from the ship's chimneys swirled across the deck, it stung the eyes and blackened the sweating skin of the sailors.

When his relief came, Ray headed for his bunk. The hot, sticky bunk room was filled with other men off duty. Cigarette smoke choked him, but he nodded a friendly greeting to his mates.

"How's our little goody-boy tonight?" A rough voice spoke from the other side of the room. John Bruning was the ship's troublemaker; he always led the persecutions of Ray.

"Aw, shut up, Bruning," Henderson growled. "Yuh can at least leave him alone."

Bruning subsided, garrulous talk continued, and the poker game went on. Ray walked across the room to his bunk, deciding to leave his clothes on, for the boat was to dock very soon.

Suddenly the loudspeaker blared, its command cutting into the hot room like a blast of cold air. "Attention, all hands. Storm approaching west-north-west. Stand by for further instructions."

Deciding that he would not be able to get any sleep, Ray headed for the top deck.

"Tom, what about the storm? Is it bad?"

"Well, Ray, Cap'n said she's supposed to be a whizzer." Tom Telgetski wiped his forehead, pushed his hair back, and set his cap straight.

"We'll make port tonight?" Ray was eager to get home again for a few hours.

"Sure, we ought'a."

Ray moved to the rail and looked out over the lake. Lightning flashed in the distance. The ship's lights made little streaks of blurred color across the waves that lapped in lulling rhythm against the side of the *Calcite*. But even as he stood there, a breeze sprang up, making the waves leap higher and lifting the heat from the atmosphere. Thunder rumbled in the distance. The roof of the sky seemed so low that he could reach up and touch it.

Ghostly clouds sailed across the moon so fast that the world seemed to be spinning.

"All hands at posts," the loudspeaker commanded. "Prepare for storm to arrive in about twenty minutes."

Men spewed forth from below deck. Each had his duty, and each hurried to perform it. Ray joined the hustling group and helped to lash down crates positioned on the deck.

John Bruning bumped Ray's shoulder, "Gonna offer a little prayer fer us tonight, Brownie? We might need it, ya know." Sarcasm oozed from his voice. Through Bruning, Satan was showing his fangs.

Ray held his temper in check. Answering quietly and courageously, he said, "I'll be glad to pray for you, John."

Bruning's thick neck grew red; the veins stood out on his sea-weathered face.

Henderson caught his arm, "None a' that, John. Come on, help me with this rope."

The wind seemed to echo Bruning's fury; it slapped faces and tossed a spray of water across the deck, drenching the sweat-soaked shirts of the men as they finished their work and hurried to don sou'westers.

Then the rain came—at first warm, but soon as cold as the lake water. There seemed no division between lake and sky: all was black; all was water. The wind blasted the ship; it blew the waves, which leaped higher and higher like wolves leaping for their prey.

Lightning flashed intermittently. Thunder crashed like cymbals in a climax of symphonic music. The ship rolled down, up, over, down, up, over. Every wave became a toboggan slide, a mountain climb, a canoe ride. Iron scraped and creaked; the *Calcite* was a complaining arthritic as she headed into the storm.

The ship's lights gleamed dimly through the pelting rain. Voices spoke and died within themselves. Through the storm the pilothouse glowed, and the shadowy form of the captain at the wheel comforted Ray as he stood in a sheltered spot, watching the forces of nature at work.

Ray left his place and dashed through the storm to the entrance leading below. Entering the bunk room, he exclaimed, "Boy, does it ever feel good in here! It's really a nasty night out."

"Ya, looks like we're in for a real dilly, Brown." Henderson glanced up from a card game. A grunt of assent came from the throats of the other men. The room retained the heat of the day, and its warmth was welcome after the chilling damp outside.

As the ship heaved, suddenly the room turned on its side. The men sprawled into a heap, the table was upset, and cards flew into the air. The *Calcite* righted herself, giving the men a chance to get their sea legs and to prepare for the next roll.

Again the ship rolled and seemed to sink like an apartment house elevator, then was caught on a wave. The propellers whirred above the noise of the storm as they left the water. The bow of the ship was caught by the next wave and balanced on its crest.

Over the din the loudspeaker roared, "Order of the captain to reverse direction. Believed dangerous to continue facing storm."

"Dangerous isn't the word for it," Tom Telgetski yelled.

Fear pushed cold fingers down the men's backs. They knew they were puppets in the hands of nature.

As the ship turned slowly about, a wave caught it broadside and sent it dipping down, down, down. In a corner the men counseled together. Ray was left alone and he fancifully wondered what he would do if they treated him as other sailors long ago had treated Jonah. Surely there were no whales in Lake Huron.

They came toward Ray—Henderson leading the group, Tom Telgetski wringing his hands, John Bruning lagging behind the others.

Swaying to keep his footing, Henderson spoke. "Ray, we know we've treated ya kinda dirty sometimes, but we want you to forgive us. An' we wanta ask a little favor of you."

Ray looked questioningly at the group; everyone was watching the tipping floor.

Then Henderson lifted his head and looked straight into Ray's eyes, "I kinda wondered if you'd pray for the *Calcite*. 'Pears like we're in pretty bad shape, an' we feel the only one kin help us is Him." Henderson gestured upward. "Ain't none of us feel like we know Him well enough to ask. Would ya do it, Ray?"

"Will you all kneel with me while we pray?" Ray asked. One by one, the sea-hardened, worldly men fell to their knees. This was a new experience for them. Bruning knelt last.

All that could be heard was the roaring of the sea, the crashing of the thunder, the groaning of the ship. Ray bowed his head and earnestly prayed—praying as one who knows his heavenly Father intimately. He finished, and the men lifted their heads and rose to their feet. Gradually the rolling decreased, and the men could balance more easily. The *Calcite* was running before the storm like a gull riding in on a wave.

A seaman burst into the room, "We'll make a harbor, guys. You can relax now. I was up in the pilothouse, and for a few minutes the captain wondered if we were going to make it or not. But, ya know, the funniest thing happened." The sailor seemed puzzled.

"What happened?" Ray demanded.

"Captain said that when the storm was at its worst that *some hand besides his* seemed to take hold of the wheel and guide the ship safely."

Amazement and wonder flickered over the faces of the listeners.

"Well, wha'da ya know!" Bruning gasped.

Knowing whose hand had guided the ship, Ray lifted his heart in thanks to God.

Dawn came like comfort after cold, like peace after pain. The *Calcite* sailed into home harbor. Each man aboard welcomed the day with thanks in his heart for the Hand on the wheel. ❧

This is one of the shortest angel stories to be taken from W. A. Spicer's The Hand That Intervenes, *and has to do with a March 8, 1849, incident of a runaway train. Train travel was still in its infancy when this wreck took place. But God's angels were watching, as this eye-opening account reveals. Isn't it significant that, where life or death are concerned, whether it was three thousand years ago or today, there is no differ-ence: one minute, you are living; another minute, you are not. Yet, have you ever wondered —I certainly have—why the vast majority of people pay so little attention to the fragility of life?*

What a sight! To see the train carrying President Taylor's inaugural address! Inconceivable that anything could hurt them if they merely watched the train go by from the safety of their front door.

To the Boston *Advent Herald* of April 21, 1849, Josiah Litch, a Philadelphia minister, contributed an article on God's providential care for His children. He said:

"I will relate an incident of recent occurrence, believing that such providences should be made public, both for the glory of God, and the edification and comfort of His children.

"Within a few rods of Trenton bridge, across the Delaware River, Pennsylvania, the New York and Philadelphia Railroad passes within about twenty feet of a block of houses, each containing four tenements, in the last of which, or the one nearest the bridge, William Kitson resides.

"On the fifth of March the government ran an express from Washington to New York to convey President Taylor's inaugural address. The family of Mr. Kitson had just finished their supper when notice was given that the express was coming, and all ran to the door to see it in its lightning flight. Mrs. Kitson, with a little girl, stepped out and stood on the steps in front of the house, while her husband and two children, one of them in his arms, stood in the doorway; and another boy went to the next door to notify them of the train's imminent arrival.

"On came the iron horse, puffing, snorting, and prancing, like a thing of life, while a stream of fire flew behind from each wheel, as it at that point pressed in a short curve upon the iron rail. It was a spectacle of terror and sublimity. I shall narrate what passed in the words of Mrs. Kitson:

" 'When I saw the engine coming, something said to me, *Run!* I said, "No, I will not; I will stand here and watch it pass." Again something said, *Run!* I said, "I won't run." Once more it sounded in my ears with such power that I could not resist it—*Run!* I then jumped from the steps, threw open the gate at the corner of the house, leading into the yard, and entered, saying at the same instant to the girl, "Run!"

" 'As soon as I had passed the gate, I turned, expecting to see the engine pass on the railroad track, but instead I saw it just behind me, coming toward the gate. It came about two-thirds of the distance from the road to the gate, directly toward the gate, and then suddenly made a sudden turn to the left, and crashed into the house!'

"Mr. Kitson, by the same invisible power which drove his wife from the steps, had been summoned from the doorway with his little boy in his arms. He had not gone the length of the door before the steps, doorway, and the side of the house were crushed. One leap just carried him beyond the door as it fell at his feet, and another leap carried him beyond the engine when it plunged into the cellar, just behind him. . . ."

In order to verify, if possible, this story of such a railway accident, we recently looked up the newspapers of that time, and the Trenton *True American* of March 8, 1849, found this news item:

"As the express locomotive came on with the President's address, a bolt broke when within a very short distance of the Delaware bridge. The locomotive ran off the track, but continued to run some distance in the direction of the road, until it reached the house of Mr. William Kitson, when it turned abruptly from the road and buried itself in the cellar, tearing away a good portion of the house." ❧

*H*ere is another synthesis from *W. A. Spicer's book,* The Hand That Intervenes; *Spicer used A. E. Glover's book* A Thousand Miles of Miracle in China *as the story source. There are enough miracles in this account to vicariously exhaust a reader. Truly, missionary work back in those days was not for the faint of heart or low of faith! One can't help but feel it was prayer warriors such as these early missionaries who planted the seeds in China that are being bountifully harvested today.*

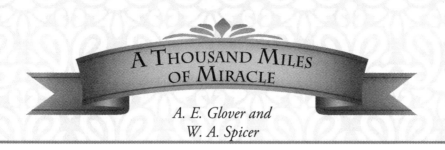

A THOUSAND MILES OF MIRACLE

A. E. Glover and
W. A. Spicer

The bloody Boxer Rebellion was raging—and hundreds of thousands of irate Chinese had had enough of the hated foreigners. Not a good time—not a good time at all—for a missionary family attempting to escape death.
It seemed impossible that they could escape mobs on all sides of them, a thousand miles from safety.

In the days of the terrible Boxer Uprising in China, in the year 1900, a missionary family was fleeing from the interior province of Shansi southward to Hankow, a thousand miles, with perils on every side.

The story of God's delivering power is told by Mr. A. E. Glover in the book *A Thousand Miles of Miracle in China.*

Only a few paragraphs can be quoted here:

The little party—Mr. and Mrs. Glover, two children, a Chinese man, and a Bible woman—had spent weary days on the road, and been robbed and stoned. Now they were prisoners in a village inn, their escort refusing to attend them farther, and the villagers filling the street and crying for the blood of the

"foreign devils," whom they held responsible for the drought and famine. The missionaries prayed for grace to meet death. But just then something happened:

"The door was pushed open, and a soldier in full uniform entered, and quietly hung his coat and cudgel on the latchet. His handsome face and commanding manner were something out of the common and could not fail to arrest attention. But this was not enough to account for the effect his sudden appearance produced upon all. I cannot describe it. It was simply startling. He was only a noncommissioned officer sent on special service to Licheng, and he was merely putting up at the inn for the night in the ordinary course of his journey—that was all.

"No, not all. Our eyes were opened to see

in him none other than God's deliverer. Even as he entered the door, he stood before us as the very angel of God. I might almost say 'a light shined in the prison,' there was something so supernatural about his presence. It was the most remarkable experience of its kind that I ever had, or my wife either; for we were both conscious of it at the same time. Not only that, but his coming produced a corresponding fear in the hearts of our enemies."

The rabble thought he must have been sent by the authorities as an official protector. The visitor was kindly disposed and agreed to lead the missionaries out of the village the next morning. That evening they had worship, and sang and prayed in the hearing of the angry crowd in the street.

"The second miracle of that memorable day followed almost immediately upon the conclusion of our worship. We had pleaded with our God to have mercy upon the people, not only in their deep spiritual need but also in their temporal distress. And we asked very definitely, in the hearing of all, that, for the glory of His great name, He would be pleased to send the rain in abundance that night, that they might know that He was the merciful God, and that we His servants were not the cause of the drought.

"Scarcely had we laid ourselves down that night, ere His voice answered from heaven in a thunder crash that shook the prison, and the rain fell in a deluge that ceased not all the night through. When morning broke, it was clear shining after rain; and the song of the Lord was in our mouths.

"The gate of our prison inn opened to us, as it were, of its own accord. Our heaven-sent soldier rode beside us and never left us all the way. No one molested us as we passed out into the road and along the highway to Shae Hsien. Indeed, we scarcely saw a soul, for at daybreak everyone had hurried to the fields to take early advantage of the long-looked-for opportunity for putting in the seed."

Later, while temporary refuge had been found at a mission station still held by a lady missionary, they were assured by the mandarin of the town of his protection.

But one day, at private prayer, Mr. Glover had Joshua 8:5 impressed upon his mind: "We will flee before them." He shrank from that word "flee," which seemed to stand out before all others with a voice of command. Could they take to the road again? But at family worship the devotional reading included 2 Samuel 15:14: "Arise, and let us flee; for we shall not else escape." And it came again like a peremptory command to hasten.

Convicted their flight was ordered by God, the refugees now began to prepare for the journey. While engaged in packing up, word came that the mandarin had been ordered to withdraw all protection; thus, they fled at midnight and escaped the slaughter that had been decreed for the day following.

On another occasion, ready to drop with fatigue, they were being driven by a mob to a temple area where they were sure to meet death. Mr. Glover says:

"We were being swept on toward the temple; and as we neared it, for the second time that dreadful day the ominous boom of the processional gong broke on our ear. At a word from Sheng-min [a Chinese Christian], we stopped and faced round.

" 'Don't go on,' he whispered. 'They mean to stone you to death there. Turn quickly.'

"As we did so, the mob hustled us severely, and with hoots and yells urged us to continue in the direction they indicated.

"It was at this most critical juncture that we experienced a really marvelous instance of God's direct interference. Sheng-min had read the peril of the moment. Knowing that we could go neither backward nor forward, he again whispered, 'Down the steep—quick! Follow the track!'

"Instantly we obeyed the direction. A thin 'goat' trail was just visible among the rocks and shrubs of the declivity; and in single file we threaded our way down, down, until at a bend in the track we were hidden from sight. Quickening our pace, we hurried on with a strength divinely renewed. In that hour we proved what it was like, in the extremity of physical weakness, to 'run, and not be weary,' to 'walk, and not faint.'

"The moment we disappeared over the side, the mob simultaneously stopped dead at the spot, as if arrested by a sudden and irresistible power. The loud yells and cries of a moment before were stilled to silence— absolute, awful silence. So startling was it that I dared to turn and take one look. I could scarcely believe my eyes. The mob lined the ridge in hundreds, motionless as if spellbound, helplessly watching us—poor, miserable us, whom they triumphantly believed they had so completely in their power—slip away from under their very eyes. Not a single soul of them attempted to follow. Sheng-min alone was behind, bringing up the rear. . . . On we sped with wondering hearts, in the consciousness that God had, for the third time at least that day, wrought for us a great deliverance."

Actual Deliverance in the Promises

Having escaped many times from those who were seeking their lives and who were yet unable to strike the blow, the fugitives took refuge one night on top of a high hill, where they hoped to hide from pursuers. Next day, they were burning up under the tropical sun, having had no water for such a long time that their tongues were indeed failing for thirst.

All the waves and billows of trouble seemed to be rolling over them at last, and Mrs. Glover sank fainting and lay prostrate and helpless on the ground. Mr. Glover says:

"As I watched her panting and gasping for breath, with no power to alleviate her suffering beyond supporting her head, it seemed as if I heard the serpent's hiss: 'Yea, hath God said? Where are His promised mercies and loving-kindness now? Has He not forgotten to be gracious?' The cruel taunt was winged to the heart of my beloved, too; and in an agony of soul she cried out from the deep darkness: 'Oh, God has forsaken us! It can only be that we are not in His will, or He would surely never have suffered us to come to this.' Her physical distress was such that I felt sure she was dying; but it was as nothing to the trouble of her soul.

"Now indeed it seemed as if the enemy's triumph was assured. The cup of sorrow was overfull; and assuming that this was the 'scourging' of the Lord, I was numb under His perceived rebuke. My heart was utterly broken before Him. But 'when the enemy shall come in like a flood, the Spirit of the Lord shall lift up a standard against him.' The moment of our deliverance was at hand. . . .

"Scarcely had the words of anguish passed my precious one's lips when God put into Miss Gates's mouth the most wonderful song of praise I have ever heard. Kneeling by the side of her prostrate sister and holding her hand, she poured forth passage after passage, promise after promise, from the Word, exalting His name, declaring His faithfulness, and proving His unchanging and unchangeable love, sworn to us in the everlasting covenant and sealed to us in the blood of His own beloved Son. Never shall I forget the music of that heavenly utterance. It was as if heaven were open above us, and the strains of the harps of God were being borne to us from glory.

"My beloved Flora drank it in—O, how eagerly!—with the avidity of a soul athirst for God, the living God. Together we drank 'out of the wells of salvation'—with what joy I cannot express—deep drafts of the pure river of water of life, flowing freely to us now from the throne of God and of the Lamb. The time had come at last for Him to reveal Himself to us. Our eyes were opened, and we knew Him; and the word of His promise was fulfilled to the letter: 'A man shall be . . . as rivers of water in a dry place, as the shadow of a great rock in a weary land.' Instantly the darkness was past, and the true light was shining again."

With stammering tongues the little party repeated to the very finish the six stanzas of the hymn:

"How sweet the name of Jesus sounds

In a believer's ear!
It soothes his sorrows, heals his wounds,
And drives away his fear."

Having found a bit of shelter in the shade, the party still tarried to escape the blazing sun, while the children were moaning for water, with tongues so swollen that they could not articulate the word. Just then came another blow: Miss Gates fainted away, and fell unconscious to the ground. Mr. Glover continues:

"It was a new and critical emergency, in the presence of which all the old helplessness came over me. As my dear wife and I were pleading with God for her recovery, I heard a word behind me as distinctly as if it were spoken in my ear: *Up, get thee down, and tarry not.* I said to my wife, 'Come, darling, we must gather up what strength remains to us, and go down to the water. It is not the will of God that we should remain here any longer.' Then, taking Miss Gates by the arm, I bent over her and said: 'Dear sister, we must be going without delay. In the name of the Lord Jesus, get up.' In a moment, consciousness was restored, and she rose up with strength renewed from on high.

"With such a confirmation that the thing was of God, and in the assurance that the Lord our God, He it was who was going before us, we left our hiding place, and once more adventured ourselves into the open. There below us, away in the not far distance, was the thin streak of silver glancing in the sunlight: the 'still waters' to which our Shepherd-Lord was leading us at last. What that sight was to our longing eyes I can never tell—the joy of pointing it out to the patient children, and of seeing the faintest smile dawn over the sad, suffering little features!

"In a few minutes, they were actually wading into midstream, lowering their lips to the stream and drinking to the full."

The Death Plots at Lanchen Cheo

And now, in their flight, Mr. Glover and his family and Miss Gates were imprisoned at Lanchen Cheo. There had been no rain in that region, and these foreign missionaries were charged with being the cause of the drought. There had been temporizing and delay, but now the cry was ringing out, "Kill! Kill! Kill!" Mr. Glover says:

"We knew well that the crisis had come, and that nothing but the direct and immediate intervention of God Himself could deliver us out of their hands. At this moment the promise was borne in powerfully upon my heart, 'Call upon Me in the day of trouble: I will deliver thee, and thou shalt glorify me.' My faith was strengthened to take hold of it, and to plead with God as a promise to which He had pledged His name, for the present hour of our trouble. Our part was to 'call upon Him;' and realizing as we did that the assigned cause of their rage against us was the long-continued drought, we were moved, under the impulse of the promise, to make a united cry to God to interfere for His great name's sake on our behalf, by sending rain enough to satisfy the needs of these poor sufferers, and because of our extremity, to send it now. Accordingly, kneeling upon the ground, we poured out our hearts before Him in Chinese, that the jailers might know exactly what we were doing and what we were asking.

"Fools! To suppose that out of a cloudless sky, as brazen as ever before, with every prospect of another day of devouring heat, rain could fall, and fall at once! Had not the guards already caught up the cry without and warned us that our hour was come—that there was not the faintest indication of rain, nor would there be until our blood had been shed? The contemptuous incredulity with which they listened showed what was in their hearts.

"How long we continued in prayer I cannot tell. I only know that scarcely had we risen from our knees when the windows of heaven were opened, and down upon the howling mob swept the sudden fury of a torrential flood of waters. In a few seconds the street was empty, and not a sound was to be heard but that swish of the rushing rain."

Even the guards were talking about the remarkable answer to the prayer of those "foreign devils." But still the missionary party was held under condemnation to death, and the officials were openly discussing their plans for taking the lives of their victims. The little missionary group determined to pray aloud in Chinese to the Lord to save them and not to permit their captors to have power over them. As they prayed, the guards outside were saying:

"They have been praying to their God to deliver them. *Ai-ia!* Deliver them indeed! Too late for that now! What is the use of praying when everything is fixed?"

The final plot devised was that of poisoning the little party that night by the introduction of opium fumes into their prison, until all should become unconscious, then to drag them out for the final stroke of death.

Everything was quiet; drowsiness overcame the party. The air became heavier and heavier. Mr. Glover found his wife and children sound asleep, and he himself was fighting the drowsiness and stupor, determined not to allow himself to fall asleep. However, it was no use, and even he pitched over into unconsciousness. He later wrote,

"The noxious fumes of the burning drug were doing their work entirely to the satisfaction of the watching jailer. The utter stillness that pervaded the prison proved it; thus, leaving his resting board, he brought the lamp in to scrutinize his victims before giving the *coup de grace*. What was his amazement to find, as he held the light to Miss Gates's face, that she was wide awake, and that upon one of the *kuei-tsi* at least the narcotic had had no power! A quick movement, designed to let him know that she was fully alive to all that was going on, so took him aback that he could only blurt out a disconcerted, '*Ai-ia!* Not asleep yet?' and withdraw to his plank and his pipe."

Morning came. All the party were recovering from the effects of the narcotic, and the keepers were discussing the experience, excusing the failure of their plot with these words:

"These people have been praying to *Shang-ti Ie-ho-hua* [Jehovah God]; and we could do nothing against their prayers."

Again the delivering hand of God opened the prison door, for the officials were apparently nonplussed and feared to do anything in the open or by daylight. Suddenly the mule driver who had deserted them two days before and betrayed them into the hands of their enemies appeared and took them out of the mob's clutches, declaring that his instructions were to take the missionaries out of Shansi. On they went toward the Shansi border, thanking God for the double deliverance that had come to save them from the death plots at Lanchen Cheo.

By the hand of Providence they were guided over the Shansi border to reach Hankow at last, truly "a thousand miles of miracle in China."

All the long way of that flight from Shansi, fanatical people were planning death for the fugitives; but day by day the blows aimed at them were warded off, and every time, when it seemed that the end had come, some delivering providence was sure to be revealed. No wonder that those who passed through these experiences of protection amid raging fury came to cling to God's promises as to a material staff of power and strength—something so real and present as almost to be handled with the hands. Again and again, on that thousand miles of flight, they heard the voice of God saying in His Word: "Call upon Me in the day of trouble: I will deliver thee, and thou shalt glorify Me."

This story comes from a very old book titled Stories Worth Re-Reading. *It looked hopeless when two little girls looked up to see a panther advancing toward them. Following the briefest of prayers, Nina "just happened" to think of having once heard that wild beasts would not attack anyone who was singing, so, hard as it was to do when trembling with fear, they did just that, and God's angels kept the girls from harm.*

The Power of Song

Nina Case

"Don't forget, girls, to start home in time to get back before dark, as many wild beasts are prowling around." Nina and Dot promised—but then forgot.

Near the summit of a mountain in Pennsylvania is a small hamlet called Honeyville, consisting of two log houses, two shanties, a rickety old barn, and a small shed, surrounded by a few acres of cleared land. In one of these houses lived a family of seven—father, mother, three boys, and two girls. They had recently moved from Michigan. The mother's health was poor, and she longed to be out on the beautiful old mountain where she had spent most of her childhood. Their household goods had arrived in Pennsylvania just in time to be swept away by the great Johnstown flood of 1889 [in which over two thousand people drowned].

The mother and her two little girls, Nina and Dot, were Christians, and their voices were often lifted in praise to God as they sang from an old hymnbook, one of their most cherished possessions.

One morning the mother sent Nina and Dot on an errand to their sister's home three and a half miles distant. The first two miles took them through dense woods, while the rest of the way led past houses and through small clearings. She ordered her daughters to start on their return home in time to arrive before dark, as many wild beasts—bears, catamounts, and occasionally a panther—were prowling around. These animals were hungry at this time of the year; for they were getting ready to "hole up," or lie down in some cozy cave or hole for their winter's nap.

The girls started off, merrily chasing each other along the way, and arrived at their sister's in good time and had a jolly romp with the baby. After dinner, the sister was so busy, and the children were so absorbed in their play, that the time passed unheeded until the clock struck four. Then the girls hurriedly started for home, hoping that they might arrive there before it grew very dark. The older sister watched until they disappeared up the road, anxiously wishing someone was there to go with them.

Nina and Dot made good time until they entered the long stretch of woods, when Nina said, "O, I know where there is a large patch of wintergreen berries, right by the road! Let's pick some for Mama."

So they climbed over a few stones and logs, and, sure enough, the berries were plentiful. They picked and talked, sometimes playing hide-and-seek among the bushes. When they finally started on again, the sun was sinking low in the west, and the trees were casting heavy shadows over the road, which lengthened rapidly. When about half the distance was covered, Dot began to feel tired and afraid. Nina tried to cheer her, saying, "Over one more long hill, and we shall be home." But now they could see the sun shining only on the top of the trees on the hill.

They had often played trying to scare each other by one saying, "O, I see a bear or a wolf up the road!" and pretending to be afraid. So Dot said: "Let's scare each other. You try to scare me." Nina said, "All right." Then, pointing up the road, she said, "O, look up the road by that black stump! I see a—" She did not finish; for suddenly, from almost the very spot where she had pointed, a large panther stepped out of the bushes, turning his head first one way and then another. Then, as if seeing the girls for the first time, he crouched down, and, crawling, sneaking along, like a cat after a mouse, he moved toward them. The girls stopped and looked at each other. Then Dot began to cry, and said, in a half-smothered whisper, "O Nina, let's run!" But Nina thought of the long, dark, lonely road behind, and knew that running was useless. Then, thinking of what she had heard her father say about showing fear, she seized her little sister's hand, and said: "No, let's pass it. God will help us." And she started up the road toward the animal.

When the children moved, the panther stopped, and straightened himself up. Then he crouched again, moving slowly, uneasily, toward them. When they had nearly reached him, and Nina, who was nearest, saw his body rising for the spring, there flashed through her mind the memory of hearing it said that a wild beast would not attack anyone who was singing. What should she sing? In vain she tried to recall some song, but her mind seemed a blank. In despair she looked up, and breathed a little prayer for help; then, catching a glimpse of the last rays of the setting sun touching the tops of the trees on the hill, she began that beautiful hymn:

"There is sunlight on the hilltop,
There is sunlight on the sea."

Her sister joined in, and although their voices were faint and trembling at first, by the time the children were opposite the panther, the words of the song rang out sweet and clear on the evening air.

The panther stopped, and straightened himself to his full height. His tail, which had been lashing and switching, became quiet as he seemed to listen. The girls passed on, hand in hand, never looking behind them. How sweet the words sounded as they echoed and re-echoed through the woods:

"O the sunlight! beautiful sunlight!
O the sunlight in the heart!"

As the children neared the top of the hill, the rumbling of a wagon fell upon their ears, so they knew that help was near, but still they sang. When they gained the top, at the same time the wagon rattled up, for the first time they turned and looked back, just in time to catch a last glimpse of the panther as he disappeared into the woods.

The mother had looked often and anxiously down the road, and each time was disappointed in not seeing the children coming. Finally she could wait no longer, and started to meet them. When about halfway there, she heard the words:

"O the sunlight! beautiful sunlight!
O the sunlight in the heart!
Jesus' smile can banish sadness;
It is sunlight in the heart."

At first a happy smile of relief passed over her face; but it faded as she listened. There was such an unearthly sweetness in the song, so strong and clear, that it seemed like angels' music instead of her own little girls'. The song ceased, and the children appeared over the hill. She saw their white faces and hurried toward them. When they saw her, how their little feet flew! But it was some time before they could tell her what had happened.

What a joyful season of worship they had that night, and what a meaning that dear old hymn has had to them ever since!

A few days later, a party of organized hunters killed the panther that had given the children such a fright. But the memory of that thrilling experience will never fade from the mind of the writer, who was one of the girls who experienced it. ❧

*U*nquestionably, this story by Gwendolen Lampshire Hayden is one of the most powerful stories in this collection. How easy it is in a freedom-loving country such as America to take freedom for granted, to assume we will always have it. Yet we know from history that nothing ever stays the same. Freedom to worship according to the dictates of one's conscience is a precious gift, and so we ought to regard it. But we learn in this story that even when things appear absolutely hopeless, if we but prayerfully ask Him, God will send His angels to watch over us.

Pay particular attention to the description of the angels and horses in this story. The story appeared both in a 1952 Youth's Instructor *and in the seventh book of Hayden's* Really Truly Stories *series.*

The Angels of Chortiza

Gwendolen Lampshire Hayden

They were lost in the maze of the forest, and at any moment their enemies might discover them. They were slowly dying of starvation, and the cold was unrelenting. If they did not somehow escape by this night—it would be too late.

Eduard crouched miserably in the back of the lumbering wagon and wondered whether he would ever again be warm. All day he had stumbled along with the tired group of men and boys who waded through the drifting snow in order that the women and children might find room on the already overcrowded cart. It was not until late afternoon that he had fallen face downward into one of the deeper drifts. Dully he recalled that he had lain there exhausted until Gerhard had lifted him up and had pushed him into the tiny space between Mother and Amalie and little Lina.

"No, no, I cannot ride," he had exclaimed thickly and with great effort. "This wagon is for the women and children. I am not a child. I must get off and walk with the men."

"You must ride, Eduard." As from a great distance he heard his kind brother-in-law's voice. "It has been many days since we have found any food to eat. All this time you have been walking. But now you are too weak to stand on your half-frozen feet. Because I once was strong I am able to keep on. But unless help comes soon I, too, will fall into the deep snow. Unless tonight we find our way out of this forest, we shall all die!"

"What is wrong, my little brother? You are not ill?" He heard the quick voice of his sister Eliesabet and saw the white blur of her thin face as she turned from the wagon seat and looked anxiously in his direction. He knew that her tired eyes could not find him among the mass of refugees crowded together into this clumsy wagon that had so miraculously fallen into their hands. Feebly he lifted his hand above his head and waved.

"I am all right, my sister. Do not worry about me. Think only of the three little girls.

They must be cared for. I am old enough to look out for myself."

The boy saw the despairing droop of his sister's shoulders and knew that she, too, was weary to the point of exhaustion. But well he realized that for them, as for the thousands of other displaced and now homeless people, there could be no rest. Neither by day nor by night could there be any rest from the enemy pursuit. Nor could there be any safety unless they soon found their way out of the dense forest in which they had become so helplessly lost.

As he slumped against the side of the rough wagon, he thought wistfully of the long-ago days when his father had been home. Then their life in the five-room white brick house had been a pleasant one, for Father and Mother had both been well and strong, and together they had made the home a happy dwelling place. In those times, they had all gathered together each morning and each evening for worship and Bible study—Father, Mother, Eduard, and the three older brothers, who had later been taken away by the invading army.

He recalled how all of them had loved the Bible. He remembered how eagerly they had searched the pages of the Holy Book for the precious truths hidden therein, even though their study had been done in secret behind the heavy wooden shutters of the double-paned windows. For in those times they dared not let it be known that they were Bible students, lest the soldiers come in the middle of the night and take away the men of the household.

Eduard's head dropped forward on his chest while in a half dream he relived the years since he was a small boy at his home in the little village on the broad, fertile plains. Again he heard the cries of his playmates as they ran merrily about in their childish games. Again he watched his father as he left early in the morning to work in the factory that was nearby.

He groaned as in memory he smelled the good odors of his mother's savory borsch. Hungrily, he pictured its tiny, tender slices of potatoes, cabbage, carrots, onions, and tomatoes floating temptingly in the rich sour-cream liquid soon to be ladled into their waiting soup bowls.

Hunger cramps cut through his empty stomach with knifelike sharpness as he recalled the delicious, nose-tickling fragrance of the loaves of crusty whole-wheat bread baking on the iron grate thrust over the glowing coals in the huge, built-in stone stove.

His ice-cold flesh throbbed painfully as once more he felt the comforting rustle of the straw mattress and the warmth of the feather-bed covering on the pull-out bench beds near the big heater. He remembered that it was here that he and his brothers had slept snug and warm through the winter temperatures of 30° to 40° below zero.

He shuddered as he thought of the dark, stormy midnight when the dreaded knock at last sounded on their door. Hot tears again burned against his eyelids as with remembering ears he heard his mother's frightened whisper, "Who's there? Who knocks on the door of Herr Heinrich?"

Eduard winced with the recollection of the harsh voice of the officer who had cried demandingly, *"Othrewaj Dweri!"* ("Open the door immediately!") and then had tramped unbidden into the shadows of the warm, candle lighted kitchen.

"Where is the man of this household? And why has he been teaching the people to turn against the government?" the officer had thundered, his fierce eyes glaring at the terrified family.

"I am the head of this household," Eduard had heard his father say bravely. "And I am guilty of no wrongdoing against the government. All these years I have worked hard to provide food for my growing family. Not once in all the long years since our ancestors came here from Holland has one of us been disloyal in any way to this country of our adoption. Ever have we kept to ourselves and tried to be good and law-abiding people. Ever have we tried to teach our children what is right and just."

"The man speaks mighty words," the officer had sneered, and Eduard had seen his thin lips tighten in anger. "But in them is there no truth. Indeed, Herr Heinrich, it has been reported that for some time have you been showing pictures—strange pictures of terrible-looking beasts that come up out of the earth. Surely, this can be nothing but a plot against our government."

"Pictures of beasts, you say?" Eduard had heard his father ask quickly. "Ah, it is concerning those that you question me in the middle of the night. Come to the table. By the light of the candle, I will show you my Bible charts, for it is of them that you speak. Here. See with your own eyes how I have drawn them from the prophecies of the Bible. I assure you there is nothing here that is in any way directed against this or any other earthly government. There is here only a pictured story of Bible history."

"You dare to speak of the Bible and yet tell us that you are not against our government?" the enraged officer had roared. Eduard had seen him clench his fists until the veins stood out against the whitened knuckles. "For one crime alone would you be exiled, but now you are guilty of two crimes. For this you shall be banished immediately."

Eduard had heard his mother's stifled moan and his father's quick indrawn breath.

"Where you are going you will have ample

time to think upon your treason. Come. Now there is no time to waste. With us you shall go this moment."

"No, no. This cannot be." Eduard had felt his eyes sting as he added his boyish, pleading voice to his mother's pitiful cry. "We have done nothing to deserve this. I swear to you that we are guilty of no wrong. Only let my father stay with us. Without his help, we cannot earn enough to eat, for already the armies are taking away our crops. Let my father remain, I beg you."

He had seen his mother fall back hopelessly as the angry officer replied to them in scorn. "Save your words, boy. Speak no more. Herr Heinrich goes with us. Let this be a lesson to all the boys in this village lest they, too, grow up to meet the fate of this man. And now we leave. There is no time to spend in idle goodbyes. Put on your coat and warm cap, Herr Heinrich. These you will need where you are going, I can promise you."

The sound of the soldier's coarse laughter had mingled with his mother's heartbroken cry and had blended into a sound that ever afterward Eduard was to hear in his frightened dreams. Ever afterward that dreadful night marked for him the beginning of a long reign of terror: his innocent father dragged away in the midnight hour, never to return; his three brothers taken away into the army and lost to their loved ones; the dreadful bombardment of the town where he had gone to live with his sister Eliesabet and her husband Gerhard when gaunt hunger had crept across the land; the eleven-day train flight over the steppes, wedged like dumb beasts into cattle cars; the horror of the two long years in the refugee camp.

The nightmare years merged together into the sharp reality of the present flight from their two-year stay in the land where they had sought asylum. Eduard opened his eyes, keenly aware of the horror of their escape before the advancing army, some of whom were even now pressing close behind them. He saw his mother's gray head bent forward upon her chest, and he prayed as he had never prayed before that somehow God would lead them out of this forest and spare their lives.

He knew that she could not stand many more days of hunger and fear. Already she and her daughter, Maria, and her daughter's children had traveled hundreds of miles from home to be reunited, almost as by a miracle, with Eduard and his sister's family. Together the little band had pressed forward, joined by other despairing refugees, until now their wagon was crowded to overflowing with its thirty-two passengers.

He listened to the heavy breathing of the two exhausted horses and the dismal screech of the wagon wheels as they plowed slowly through the fresh-fallen snow. He shivered as the wintry northern wind cut through his thin clothing and slashed into his quivering flesh. Again the keen pangs of hunger gripped him as he tried dully to recall how many days it had been since he had had any food.

But I mustn't think about that, he thought despairingly. *I mustn't. I've got to be strong and brave, so that I can help my sister with her three little girls. Already the weather has become so cold that baby Anni has almost frozen in the little nest of straw that we have made for her here in the wagon. Soon it will be night, and we will be unable to travel any farther, for we are lost. Some of us who are stronger will have to stay awake and seek for some way out of this forest, else we will all perish and the wolves will pick our bones clean and white.*

Already Gerhard has told me that our lives depend upon finding our way to safety this very night. And he has said that without the Lord's help, we are doomed to die. Indeed, I know well that we cannot live through the bitter darkness without food or shelter of some kind, for it has been days since we have eaten or rested.

"O God," he prayed, "I know that Thou dost still watch over us. I know that Thou has spared our lives and brought us this far in our flight from danger. May our guardian angels be by our sides and lead us in safety from this dense forest. Answer our prayers, O God. Answer our prayers, and we will give Thee all the glory and honor forever. Amen."

"Listen."

Eduard raised his head, startled by Gerhard's low voice. He saw that everyone else had also roused and that every face was turned fearfully toward the right, listening, listening to the distant sound borne on the rising wind.

"O Gerhard, what is it?" he heard Eliesabet gasp. "Is it—do you think the soldiers—oh, what shall we do! What *shall* we do!"

"I know not what it is, but I fear for the worst," he heard Gerhard's slow reply. "Yet there is nothing that we can do but continue to pray. Let us stop and lift our hearts to God. Let us ask that His protecting hand may be stretched over us to blot us from the sight of our enemies and to lead us from this great forest.

"Surely, the beautiful words of the psalms are as true today as in the days of old, for we know that the same God rules yesterday, today, and forever. He has promised that 'he shall cover thee with his feathers, and under his wings shalt thou trust. . . . Thou shalt not be afraid for the terror by night; . . . nor for the pestilence that walketh in darkness. . . . There shall no evil befall thee, neither shall any plague come nigh thy dwelling. For he shall give his angels charge over thee, to keep thee in all thy ways. They shall bear thee up in their hands, lest thou dash thy foot against a stone.' But let us continue to trust our God, Eliesabet. Then, come what may, we shall be in His care and keeping. And now, loved ones, let us pray together before we press onward in the gathering darkness."

Eduard never forgot the majestic sound of the Lord's Prayer as it arose from the pale, chilled lips of the weary refugees who pressed close together and humbly bowed their heads.

"Unser Vater im Himmel! Dein Name werde geheiligt!

Dien Reich komme. Dein Wille geschehe auf Erden wie in Himmel.

Unser täglich Brot gib uns heute.

Und vergib uns unsere Schulden, wie wir unsern Schuldigern vergeben.

Und führe uns nicht in Verschung, sondern erlöse

Uns von dem übel. Denn dein ist das Reich und die

Kraft und die Herrlichkeit in Ewigkeit. Amen."

He never forgot the earnestness of the weak voices as they prayed in utter faith and asked that God would that very night lead them to safety and to shelter. And he never forgot the shock of Gerhard's hoarse unexpected call at the conclusion of their brief prayer meeting.

"Halloo, I say!" Again he heard his brother-in-law's voice. "Who are you, stranger, and can you help us? For we are hopelessly lost in these woods and cannot make our way to safety."

In the gathering dusk, Eduard strained his eyes to see to whom Gerhard was pointing. A thrill ran down his back as he saw the dim outlines of two men, each seated on a white horse, each waiting silently for the wagon to move close to them. He noted wonderingly that the beautiful animals stood as though carved in white marble until, in response to some unseen signal, they moved forward with a silent fluid motion unlike any he had ever seen.

"Wait, strangers. Can you show us the way? Answer me, I beg of you." Again he heard Gerhard's imploring question. Again he saw the white horses stop and then move slowly forward in one common impulse. Their movement was the only answer to Gerhard's question, for their silent riders did not speak but only pointed straight ahead.

"Are you going to follow where they lead us?" he heard his sister ask fearfully. He sensed the tearful note in her voice, and knew that she feared possible betrayal into the hands of the enemy. "O Gerhard, stop. Perhaps this is a trap, and we will all be captured and killed," she half sobbed.

"Then it is a chance that we must take, Eliesabet," came Gerhard's low reply. "The little children and the older people will freeze to death if we stay here another night, for we have no warm clothing and no bedding. They cannot endure this biting cold or the cruel pangs of hunger for many more hours.

"But somehow I cannot believe that this is another trick of the enemy. Somehow I cannot believe that God will permit us to die after leading us this far. Deep in my heart is the conviction that these men wish us well and that they will help us. Let us continue to trust in God and to pray that He will deliver us from 'the snare of the fowler.' "

Eduard noted the sudden silence that fell upon the group of weary, homeless ones pressed close against him. No one spoke aloud, but all prayed silently as the thin, tired horses labored through the night. Again the exhausted children slept as the worn wheels creaked against the glittering snow crystals that sparkled frostily in the light of the newly risen, cold, pale moon.

On and on through the long night hours the pilgrimage wound its way among the trees. On and on they rode, unquestioningly following the white-robed horsemen just ahead. Wonderingly, Eduard noted that no sound betrayed the movement of the beautiful white animals. Wonderingly, he saw that no steaming breath could be seen ascending from their flaring red nostrils.

On and on and on. Eduard marveled at the sure, steady guidance of the strangers. Well he knew that none of his refugee party could have found his way from the maze of trees into which they had fled in their headlong escape from the pursuing army. And well he knew that without the help of these kindly strangers, his forlorn group was doomed to die. He tried to think how far they had come in their long flight from fear—how far— how very far—how very, very far—

"Pr-r-r!" ("Whoa!")

Eduard roused with a jerk and stared wildly about him. He saw that in the east the first faint red light of the dawn was painting the cold gray sky and touching the white sleeping world with that mysterious light for which there is no description. His sleepy eyes looked back at the green forest crowding close behind them and then ahead at the two white horses standing directly in front of their wagon. He listened to Gerhard's excited voice as he turned and urged the passengers to wake.

"Look, friends," he cried joyfully. "At last we are out of the dreadful woods. At last we are on our way to safety, far from the pursuing soldiers. All night have these kind strangers led us through the deep forest. All night have they led us to this very spot and pointed ahead to a path that is safe for travel.

"Indeed, they have even led us to food and shelter, for close behind us is a hurriedly deserted house. And in it has one of our group found not only loaves of bread and a large can of syrup but also some torn quilts, which we can wrap around the children and the old folks.

"Truly, we can never thank these men enough for their great goodness. But at least we can try to do so, each and every one of us."

Quickly, Eduard once again turned his eyes toward the silent, mysterious riders and prepared to call out the thankful words that pressed against his lips. But the message died unspoken, and he felt weak and breathless and half-afraid as he stared about him. For, though he looked in every direction, he could see no trace of the two white horses or the two riders who had only a moment before rested in front of their wagon.

"Quick, Gerhard," he gasped. "Be quick. The men have gone. Oh, where could they be? Why, they were standing right there as you began speaking. I saw them as plainly as I see you, and *you* haven't vanished. Surely, they must have turned to the left and again entered the forest. Let us hurry to catch up with them and give them our heartfelt thanks. We must tell them of our gratitude."

Eduard knew that he would never forget the strange feeling of awe that swept across him as he saw Gerhard's weary face begin to glow with light and warmth.

" 'He withdraweth not his eyes from the righteous.' 'He delivereth the poor in his affliction,' " he said solemnly, triumphantly.

"Surely, the Lord has been in this place, and we knew it not. All night long we have traveled through a forest infested with soldier spies. Many times I saw the glow of a distant campfire and heard the roar of rough laughter. Yet not once were any of those soldiers permitted to hear the sound of our creaking wagon or the laboring breath of our almost exhausted horses. Surely, our guardian angels who were by our side in our home have been with us all along the way.

"Are we not told to 'be not forgetful to entertain strangers: for thereby some have entertained angels unawares'? Truly, this day our eyes have beheld a miracle!"

And as Eduard looked from Gerhard's face to the fresh, unbroken snow that lay spread out in front of them, he knew that on this morning those Bible truths had once again been fulfilled. He knew that God had indeed sent His angels to lead them in safety so that their lives might be spared. And in his heart, he determined anew that, come what might, he would always be faithful to the One who had so miraculously delivered them. ❧

SECTION FOUR

FOR HE SHALL GIVE HIS ANGELS CHARGE OVER THEE, TO KEEP THEE IN ALL THY WAYS. THEY SHALL BEAR THEE UP IN THEIR HANDS, LEST THOU DASH THY FOOT AGAINST A STONE.
PSALM 91:11, 12 (KJV)

*E*very time I read this story, I keep seeing a double-exposure of the time an out-of-control pickup driver, having lost his trajectory, veered across the yellow line and smashed into us. When both my wife and I assumed that this was it—that our lives were over. And just as was true with Dixil Rodríguez's car, when people saw the wreckage of our car, they couldn't believe we weren't dead or incapacitated for life. I'd guess that many of you have had similar experiences, or known others who have. Invariably, the response is, "Your guardian angel really works overtime!" or "Somebody up there was surely watching over you!"

I'm sure the story's author will agree with me when I say, "Ever after such a close call, we take each new day as a serendipitous gift from God, recognizing that we are living on borrowed time. For some unexplainable reason, God wasn't through with us yet—our journey on this earth was not yet over. Not yet was it the 'last day of our lives.' " This story appeared in a *2008* Adventist Review.

THE CALLING CARD

Dixil L. Rodríguez

All is as usual in her commute to work—until everything that can go wrong suddenly does. Death stares her in the face.
Then . . .

I have a dear friend who teaches literature. One day over lunch, she tells me about a research project she is working on. It involves calling cards.

The practice of calling cards has been in place for centuries. A calling card can be a piece of paper with a family seal on it, or a card imprinted with a person's name in beautiful calligraphy. My friend tells me the calling card of long ago was elegant and was meant to inform those residing in a home that a visitor had come to see them. It was also, at times, a reminder of a loved one come to visit.

I gently remind her we still have calling cards today, but now we call them business cards. She smiles and says, "They're different. When I extend my business card, I am in essence saying, 'I am here to conduct a transaction, collect money, discuss business—so

here's my business card.' " But a calling card, she explains, presented only the name of the individual, and it carried value in the form of a simple connotative phrase: *"I came to see you."*

This conversation with my friend was light and friendly, easily forgotten. But a life-changing experience later brought it forcefully to mind.

Just Another Day?

I love my job. Teaching is what I do best. I commute about thirty miles every morning to Tarrant County College in Fort Worth, Texas. It's a wonderful commute; I am against the rush-hour traffic. Often I am fortunate enough to catch the sunrise.

The commute today is no different until I am about halfway to my destination and hear an unfamiliar noise. The tire on the front driver side of my car has been punctured. I hear metal scraping on the road, and I know I am in trouble. Frantically, I look to my right and see vehicles. My brakes are not working. I attempt to steer off the road, but the steering wheel has lost power. I am heading straight over the bridge ahead at an angle at which I will certainly hit the concrete median that separates the bridge from the space below. I hear myself say, "Dear God, not today!"

What follows is a blur. I hit the median, and the car spins in circles. The scraping noise gets louder and louder; the spinning car keeps slamming against something hard—the bridge. Suddenly, something hits my face, and everything goes black!

Help From a Stranger

"Ma'am, don't move; you've had a bad wreck."

I hear the voice of someone talking to me through my driver's window. The car appears to be full of smoke. My right hand seems to be glued to the steering wheel. Using my left hand, I try to open the door to get out. It doesn't budge. I begin to scream, believing my car is burning and I am stuck in it.

"Ma'am, you are fine. There is no fire," the man says. "My buddy and I just parked our pickup trucks across the way. No traffic is going to hit you. He's gonna try to open the

passenger door for the smoke to get out. It's not really smoke; it's just that the air bags deployed."

I don't know whose voice it is, but I am grateful for it. In a moment, I see someone open my passenger door. Already he's on the phone calling 911. He looks at me while talking into the phone.

"No, she's not bleeding. There are no open wounds," he says.

My head hurts. I wonder, *Who is he?* My driver side door is being opened. I see the man who has been talking to me. He must be about forty years old. Sunburned. He has a cast on his right hand. I wonder how he got hurt. He squats next to the vehicle and gently places his hand, the one with the cast on it, over my own.

"What's your name?" he asks.

My name? Why does he want my name? I wonder. I just stare at him. I am aware I am wheezing. I don't know where my asthma medication is; I don't know where my purse is.

"You had a bad accident," the man says. "You probably got hit pretty hard with the air bag. Did you black out?"

Black out? It starts to make sense. I say "Yes" to the stranger. But I can't say anymore because of my difficulty breathing.

"It's OK," he says. "You are OK. You are safe. Your tire blew out, and you lost control of the vehicle. We were right behind you, and we stopped traffic. We watched your car spin out of control and the air bags come out. You are lucky those are concrete barriers or you would have been over the bridge. Can you remember your name?"

I can! I can remember! I think to myself. *I can say it. But I need to remember to breathe.*

"Dixil," I tell him. *Breathe.* "I teach. I am going to work." *Breathe.* "I have a training session I need to attend." *Breathe, breathe.* The air feels like water just leaking out of my lungs.

"Dixil, we have to regulate your breathing, OK, because the medics aren't here yet." I feel the stranger pat my hand. "I just need you to relax for a minute. Breathe regularly. That's good—just breathe."

He keeps talking about some accident. Oh, his accident. He just broke his hand in a car accident last week.

The air bags lie flat on my windshield. The windshield is cracked.

I feel the stranger take my pulse. Just barely, but I feel it. The ambient noise is so loud. I hear ambulances or the police.

"You are very fortunate," the stranger says. "And your tires don't look like they should be shredding like that; they look almost new."

I realize my breathing is much better. So does he.

"That's good," he says, and pats my hand as he goes through the motion of slow breathing with me.

Medical Help Arrives

The emergency medical technicians (EMTs) are approaching us, carrying a yellow board that looks very stiff. One of them carries a collar. I know he will put it on me. My whole body feels like it was crushed in concrete.

"It's not going to hurt," my friend says. "They will put the collar on you, and it will facilitate getting you out."

The EMTs quickly put a neck collar on me and strap me onto the hard yellow board. My friend tells them: "I think she has some ribs broken on both the right and the left, and she is hyperventilating. She has asthma, and the smoke made her cough. She's been wheezing a lot."

I can't remember telling him I had asthma.

The EMTs take me into the ambulance where they begin an assessment. Lights are coming at me . . . masks. . . . I see an IV bag being handed across me. I hear them talking to me. Their voices are soft.

"Can you feel this?" they ask. "Does this hurt when I press here? Can you follow the light?"

I can't see my car anywhere, but in the distance I can see the traffic backup. *Oh, no! I didn't mean for* that *to happen.*

A cop comes into the ambulance and talks to me. He tells me there is no citation or violation of traffic laws. Many witnesses saw what happened. I look at him; he looks very kind. I feel better. Maybe they will let me get out of the ambulance and go home.

I apologize to him for the traffic backup. He laughs and then says, "Lady, have you seen your car? It's a miracle you are alive."

He hands one of the EMTs his business card and instructs him to make sure I keep it because it will tell me where to find my car. Then he looks at me again and says, "You say a special prayer tonight. People don't walk away from an accident like this. Not without a body bag."

He adds, "I'm taking your car to the impound in Fort Worth."

Getting His Name

My friend with the broken hand approaches the ambulance carrying my purse, my laptop, and my book bag. I was wondering about those items. He hands them to the police officer and says, "Here, she needs these. Her cell phone is tagged to her purse. She's got family close by."

I do? I do. My mother is visiting from Maryland and staying with my sister and niece in Burleson. When did I say this to him?

There is a pause as they arrange the packages inside the vehicle, then my friend says, "Dixil, you take it easy now. You stay clear off those dangerous roads, professor."

The police officer begins to exit the ambulance, and I realize I never asked who my attentive companion was.

"Officer," I whisper, "that man who brought my bag. I don't know his name. I want to thank him. Who is he?"

The officer yells out to the stranger, "Hey, buddy, the lady would like to say thank you. Is there a name I can give her?" The officer walks over to the man and returns with a business card. He places it in the front pocket of my computer bag. Doors are about to shut, but I hear words from the stranger that I cannot erase from my mind: "Tell her Puppy says she'll be fine."

There's a silent moment as one of the EMTs takes my blood pressure again, then he says, " 'Puppy,' what kind of name is that? Is that what that guy called himself?"

A memory is stirred.

Grateful for Protection

About six hours later, I am done with the hospital. My friend was right; I have cracked ribs. Three on one side, two on the other. My wrist is bruised as well. Everyone tells me how lucky I am. On the drive home, I insist we stop by the police impound where the remains of my car have been towed. I need to recover my students' papers. My family doesn't protest.

As we inch our way through the lot, I notice one of the vehicles. My mother notices it too. "That looks terrible!" she says. It had my license plate stuck to the trunk. We stop. Everything has changed. Looking at the wreck, I can better understand why everyone was amazed. I start crying. There is nothing recognizable here.

We quietly collect the items we find and head home. The drive is quiet. I tell my mother about the stranger who helped me. "Look," I say. "He left me a business card. I'm going to call and thank him."

My mother looks at the card. There's not much there. There's the name: "Puppy." There is a phone number under the name. Then under the name, a slogan: "We care for people."

Then, I remember.

A Childhood Experience

I don't know exactly how old I was. I remember playing outside in the yard with my sister. She was riding her bike across the front porch when she lost control of it, and I watched in terror as her bike slid toward the edge of a significant drop at the end of the patio. I remember hearing her say something like, "Susan, don't let me go!"

Susan was her guardian angel. My sister had named her guardian angel. I decided I would do the same. *But what would I call my angel?* I thought. Nothing came to mind. Right then, most of my life was preoccupied with a puppy that one of our neighbors had. He was so cute.

Puppy! That could be a name!

A Calling Card?

No listing exists for my friend. No Internet search has pulled his name up. The phone number on the card had been disconnected, and there is no forwarding number. No phone operator has been able to help me. The card is ripped at the corner, worn and jagged. I am certain it was not kept in a business card folio. This card was in someone's pocket, placed there as an afterthought while getting dressed. Yet here it is now, in my hand.

A business card? A calling card?

Either way, it meant *"I came to see you."* ❧

This story from a 1937 Youth's Instructor *reminds me very much of Lois Wheeler Berry's story, "He Shall Give His Angels Charge Over You" in section three. As you read this story, you can vicariously feel that angelic force that suspends natural law and thus enables the cyclist to safely make it around that deadly curve. In literature, we would label such an act within a story as* deus ex machina—*a force outside the story flow, with the power to alter the outcome from what would have occurred under natural law.*

What a God we serve!

UNDERNEATH

Martin Pascoe

John Gordon dreaded that bicycle ride to town—mainly because of that unbelievably slippery steep grade with a nasty turn three hundred feet above Rocky Creek. What if he'd lose control on that grade? What if he'd lose his brakes?
All went well—until . . .

Well, goodbye! I am going now. I have a long way to ride into town and the meeting starts at three o'clock," said young John Gordon to his wife, as he buttoned his overcoat and buckled the belt.

"Goodbye, John," she responded a little anxiously. "I do wish the road were not so wet and slippery. It will be dangerous down that second hill, after all this rain, won't it? I hope you get there all right, and have a good meeting in New Plymouth."

"Don't worry," her husband assured her quietly; "I will be very careful, and my brakes are good. God's angels will protect us both. Bye, dear."

John Gordon pulled his hat on firmly and drew the belt of his coat a little tighter as he stepped out with his bicycle into the drizzling rain. Fifteen miles he had to go. The last five would be right across the plain, but the first ten might not be so easy, winding down the foothills of Mount Egmont. And the first two miles! He hated even to think of that second hill which led down to Rocky Creek, it was so steep, so slippery. And that dangerous sharp bend a hundred yards above the gully!

He was nearly halfway down the first hill now, and the rain was stopping. The bicycle ran smoothly, and his foot brake held the wheel back easily. In a few minutes, he was climbing the next rise. Up, up, he pushed; then as the road became steeper, he got off and walked. It was muddy here, and very slippery.

In a few minutes, he gained the top of the second hill. Looking down, he could see the road descending very sharply for nearly half a mile. Then there was that bad bend, where the road was cut out of the side of the rock three hundred feet above Rocky Creek, and after that a straight run to the bridge. What would happen if his wheels skidded on the clay surface as he went down? "The brakes are good, and will hold anywhere," he tried to reassure himself, "and if the hand brake gets too wet, the foot brake will hold. But suppose both brakes should—"

He dared not think of it!

Soon he was descending the hill. The hand brake was slipping badly, and the wet rims were becoming more slippery. Faster, faster, the bicycle was going. The foot brake would be better. *What a comfort to have a reliable foot brake!* he thought as he reversed the pedals.

Just then, a little spring somewhere in his back wheel snapped. Oh! Horror! His foot brake had given way. He went faster, faster! Neither brake would act now, and the grade was becoming steeper. Down, down, he raced. Fifty yards farther was that dreadful bend. What could he do?

Clinging to that bolting bicycle on the slippery, dangerous mountainside, John Gordon gasped an urgent prayer. "Jesus, help!" he pleaded. Maybe his wife, back in their little home, was just then praying for him, too. But his terrific pace was unchecked.

His heart almost stood still as he approached the bend. Above the whistling of the wind, he could hear the roaring creek, hundreds of feet below. He could *never* get round that corner at this speed! Nothing on earth could stop him now from going over that cliff. He was shooting toward the edge.

And then the miracle happened.

He felt a light touch about his waist, not a heavy hold, but a very gentle pressure on either side. The bicycle had lost its terrible weight; he himself felt as light as a feather. Was he dreaming? Could he really be rounding that elbow? Yes, straight ahead was the bridge, and he was racing down again toward it. He was safe.

The mad pace had ceased by the time he had crossed the bridge, and soon he was able to stop. Reverently thanking God for his escape, and leaving his bicycle at the bridge, he climbed up again to the bend. All the way he could trace his tracks till he came within a few yards of the bend. There the tire prints in the clay ceased abruptly. He walked around the bend, searching for tire prints, but found none. A few yards above it, he found marks again, ending as sharply as those on the lower side. For a distance of at least twenty-five feet, the tires had evidently not touched the ground!

Right on the bend of a narrow road, three hundred feet above the roaring, tumbling Rocky Creek near the foot of Mount Egmont, a young man might have been seen that late afternoon, pouring out his heartfelt praise to God whose everlasting arms are ever "underneath," and whose angel "encampeth round about them that fear Him, and delivereth them." ❧

*H*ere is another of the stories W. A. Spicer preserved for us in The Hand That Intervenes. *It means even more to me because as a historian, I'm familiar with Frederick William III and his lovely queen, Louisa. How everything seemed to go well for them until Napoleon decided he wanted to rule all Europe. One of the obstacles in his way was Prussia. He defeated it, treating its monarchs as so much trash. One of the stories that has long haunted me has been when Queen Louisa took it upon herself to try to save her people: she took a long trip to where Napoleon was temporarily residing and entreated Napoleon to have mercy on her people. Napoleon, in essence, sneered at her and spurned her plea, and she sadly returned to her husband and family. It is said that she died of a broken heart. And just to show how life has a way of coming full circle, when France was invaded by Germany in 1870 and thoroughly humiliated, it was no small thanks to the bitterness Germany still held against Napoleon's treatment of their queen.*

But all that is just a side story to the one in this book, when God set up the king to be receptive to a now repentant count, who had attempted to kill Frederick William. Doesn't this story remind you of similar ones in the Bible?

The count, a wicked and godless man, had attempted to kill his king, but was caught in time. Now, in solitary confinement, with a storm without and a storm within, he picked up the Book . . .

A count who had plotted against Frederick William III of Prussia, even attempting personal violence, was imprisoned in the fortress of Glatz, Upper Silesia. His story, translated from the practical commentaries of Dr. Besser, pastor of Waldenburg, was printed in the Boston *Christian*. The count had no other reading material than a Bible, which he was in no mood to open, as he was opposed to religion. But after a long time of solitary confinement, he began to read the Book. Gradually, it touched his life. The account says:

"On a rough, stormy November night, when the mountain gales howled round the fortress, the rain fell in torrents, and the swollen and foaming Neisse rushed roaring down the valley, Count of M—— lay sleepless on his cot. The tempest in his breast was as fearful as that without. His whole past life rose before him, and he was convicted of his man-

ifold shortcomings and sin; he felt that the source of all his misery lay in his forsaking God. For the first time in his life his heart was soft, and his eyes wet with tears of genuine repentance.

"He rises from his cot, opens his Bible, and his eye falls on Psalm 50:15: 'Call upon Me in the day of trouble: I will deliver thee, and thou shall glorify Me.' This word of God reaches to the depths of his soul; he falls on his knees for the first time since he was a child and cries to God for mercy; and that compassionate God who turns not away from the first movement of faith toward Him heard the cry of this sufferer in the storm-beaten dungeon of Glatz and gave him not only spiritual but temporal deliverance."

And this is how the deliverance came, by the providence of God:

"The same night [of the count's surrender], in his castle at Berlin, King Frederick

William III lay sleepless in bed. Severe bodily pains tormented him, and in his utter exhaustion he begged of God to grant him a single hour of refreshing sleep. The favor was granted; and when he awoke again, he said to his wife, the gracious Louise, 'God has looked upon me very graciously, and I am thankful to Him. Who in my kingdom has wronged me most? I will forgive him.'

" 'The Count of M——,' replied Louise, 'who is imprisoned in Glatz.'

" 'You are right,' said the sick king; 'let him be pardoned.'

"Day had not dawned over Berlin ere a courier was dispatched to Silesia, bearing to the prisoner in Glatz pardon and release." ❧

*I*t was a number of years ago when Teresa Sales sent me this moving story. It has remained in our story archives ever since, waiting for its time. It's interesting, is it not, to see how many individuals have had confirmed validity of their suspicions that a rescuer was an angel, by the presence or absence of tracks in snow, mud, or dirt. This 1958 story has been in the hopper for a good many years as well!

WHITEOUT!

Teresa Sales

It just didn't make any sense: driving into the heart of a blizzard rather than waiting it out.
But strangely, she was convicted that they should make the dangerous trip anyway.
Why, she just didn't know.
But haven't we all experienced such situations?
Convictions so strong that, even when they appear to make little sense,
we still feel, for some inexplicable reason, that we have to do it.
Later, we find out why.

*I*t's time, I thought to myself. *It's time to head for the nearest hospital.*

Two weeks earlier, a doctor had attempted to induce labor unsuccessfully. Even though I wasn't experiencing any pains yet, I was certain our first baby was ready to be born.

It was the fall of 1958, and there were no hospitals in the west end of Montrose County, Colorado. Employees at the uranium plants in Uravan and Naturita had access to company doctors, and some women—braver than myself—used them to deliver their babies. But my husband, Don, was teaching school and pastoring in a small log church in Nucla. We had to find other medical help. Not even our parents lived close by.

"Are you sick to your stomach? Has there been any kind of discharge?" My husband alternated between asking questions from Dr. Spock and the other health book we owned and glancing anxiously out the window at the threatening weather. He wanted to be sure I was reading my symptoms correctly before we headed toward the mountain pass that separated us from Montrose.

I had to honestly answer "No" to each of his questions. But I was sure we needed to leave for the hospital as soon as possible.

We quickly packed what few baby things we had—two diapers, a sleeper, some receiving blankets—in an old suitcase. Filled with the soft blankets, the suitcase would double as a baby crib on the way home.

As we drove down the two-block main street of the small mining town, we stopped at the barber shop to see if the barber's wife wanted to accompany us. Expecting her fourth child at any moment, she had been hoping this time to have the baby in a real hospital, where she could rest before returning home.

Looking at the sky that was clouding over rapidly, she sighed. "I'll try to wait out the storm. Are you sure you want to go today?"

"I'm sure," I said. *But I don't know why. Please, God, give us a safe journey—for us and our unborn child.*

The first few miles were easy driving, but long before we reached Dallas Divide, we knew we were in trouble. Huge clusters of snowflakes began piling up on the windshield, accumulating too fast for the wipers to remove them.

No Turning Back

We slowed to a crawl, peering out the window, trying to see ahead of us and keep far from the road's edge. If we slipped, an icy river waited below. Everything seemed lost in time in a quiet, but deadly, environment.

Hours later, we made it through the canyon and down the dangerous divide. But as we reached Ridgeway, sixty-three miles from

home, dusk was falling and visibility was zero. We were caught in a total whiteout.

"We can't go any farther," my husband said as we inched our way toward the junction of the highway to Montrose. The town was another twenty-six miles.

He's right, I thought. *Why do I feel we need to be at the hospital today? We can't see beyond the front of the car. The road has disappeared completely in the snow. And we haven't seen another vehicle for miles.*

Ridgeway offered few amenities at that time: no hospital, no motel—even if we could have afforded one. It had only a few houses and a gas station.

As we cautiously approached the Montrose junction, we saw the taillights of a vehicle ahead pulling onto the highway. We assumed it came from the gas station in Ridgeway.

I felt an immediate sense of relief. "Look, honey," I said. "That looks like a pickup heading toward Montrose. Let's follow the taillights into town." Don agreed to try.

Driving by Faith

It's so strange, I said to myself. *Nothing looks familiar.* Although we had made the trip many times, the blizzard obliterated any landmarks, anything that would put our minds at ease. We could not see anything in front, behind, or to either side of us.

Except the taillights.

We followed those two lights slowly, but with a sense of confidence that the driver ahead of us knew the road better or could see it better than we could. *Or somehow knew how badly we needed his guidance,* I thought.

The last grueling miles seemed the longest, but finally we saw the lights of Montrose shining through the heavily falling snow.

As we reached the town and were able to get our bearings from familiar structures, the vehicle in front of us turned down a side street.

"Where did it go?" I asked. My husband pulled over and got out to look. The street lights provided enough illumination to see part way down the street.

But the truck had vanished in the snowfall—leaving no tire tracks on the street where we had seen it turn.

We looked at each other in awe but continued to a pastor friend's home where we had arranged to stay until the baby came. My water broke as soon as we entered our friend's door, so we immediately drove to the hospital.

The labor was long and intense, not unusual for a first child. But I kept thinking about the unusual circumstances of the trip that realistically shouldn't have been taken. *Why had I felt such urgency?*

After delivering our son, the doctor looked at me and said quietly, "It's a good thing you made it to the hospital. The baby's cord was wrapped tightly around his neck. If you'd had him on the road, he wouldn't have lived. You were lucky."

No, it wasn't luck, I thought. *It was God's hand leading us and our newborn to safety in the storm.* ❧

*E*llsworth Schneider's story was published in a 1943 Youth's Instructor. *I can testify from personal experience that revolutions are anything but a laughing matter. How well I remember one in Guatemala during my growing-up years. During a revolution, all civil control ceases, for no one is in charge. It so happened that when the Guatemala revolution began, my father and the mission president, Melvin Sickler, were in the interior in the mission Jeep. Since they were due to arrive home the day the revolution began, we made his safety the subject of near continual prayer. When Dad failed to return, we worried even more. Three days later, what a story they had to tell! The day they were to return home, their mission Jeep got stuck in a massive mudhole. Since the rain continued to fall, they were unable to extricate it for three long days. By the time they'd finally been pulled out, though the revolution still raged, they were able to make it safely into Guatemala City. They were told that had they attempted to enter the capital city three days before, they'd be dead, for the soldiers were shooting first and asking questions afterwards. As for the Jeep, it would have automatically been considered military and hence disposed of quickly. So we've always felt God's angels made sure that Jeep remained stuck in the mudhole for three days.*

In the case of this particular story, notice the interaction of the out-of-control mobs and the angels attired in white suits. One of the fascinating aspects of angels, in angel accounts, is that never is their authority challenged! Clearly, the Divine represents such a force field that resistance to it is not even possible.

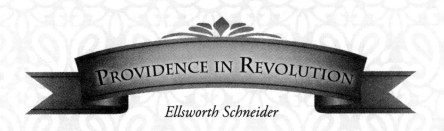

PROVIDENCE IN REVOLUTION

Ellsworth Schneider

Boom! Boom! Boom! roared the cannons. Ta-ta-ra-ra-ra-ta went the rifles and machine guns not so very distant from where we lived. Soon we heard cries from people who were running through the streets. Revolution! The revolution had broken out!

My father was away from home at the time on a trip inland. As soon as trouble broke loose, he realized there was great danger, not only for him but for his family, from whom he was separated by a distance which would require two weeks of travel by the fastest transportation available. He had received word that the last boat, a very small one, was leaving within an hour. It would try to run the enemy blockade and reach the city in which we lived. Communications were severed. The mail no longer came through. Conditions remained thus for six months, leaving everyone in a world by himself.

My father hurriedly packed his belongings and started across town to the docks. Since the streetcars were no longer running, he looked for a taxi. Unable to find one, he started to walk, knowing very well he would never make it in time for the departure of the boat. To his surprise, he met a taxi. He jumped in the car and asked the driver to take him across town faster than he had ever gone before. The driver looked astonished and said he would not move his car. Besides, it would be pure suicide to attempt to drive across town. Large mobs had already gathered and were destroying homes, offices, and stores, and killing everyone they thought might have anything to do with the government.

But it is possible to do almost anything with money in that country, and the driver finally consented to drive to the docks. However, he still refused to go through town and insisted on a very roundabout way which would take them far into the country.

The race began. There was only a half hour left. The taxi moved as fast as possible on the narrow, bumpy dirt road. They were making good progress when, rounding a corner, they observed a large gathering off in the distance. The driver immediately slowed down, planning to turn back.

With much coaxing and pleading and a final assurance that it would be entirely his own risk, Father persuaded him to go on. Coming nearer to the mob, they noticed that the men were armed with all sorts of implements of destruction which they were swinging in the air. They made a great deal of noise, shouting and cursing. By now it was impossible to turn back, so they went on. Father prayed constantly that they might get through safely to the docks and eventually reach home.

The mob, which was stopping all cars to see whether there were any government officials trying to escape, had already noticed the approaching taxi. Gathering in the streets and blocking it completely, they pointed their weapons toward the oncoming car and motioned it to stop.

The driver knew very well what would happen if he did stop, for that same day he had seen two of his companions go off with passengers and met them when they came back with no car left and a terrifying tale to tell of how the angry mobs had killed their passengers.

He gritted his teeth and stepped on the accelerator, intending to plow straight through the crowd, since he could think of nothing better to do. When the mob saw the car was not going to stop, each person forgot all he was going to do and thought only of saving his own life. By swerving and skillful driving, the man got through without hurting anyone. On they sped, hoping against hope that they would not encounter any more difficulty.

Suddenly, clouds of dust appeared in the distance. They could make out many people indistinctly as if they were behind a smoke screen. To their dismay, it was another mob. This time it was larger, stronger, and more angry. Apparently, they had had previous experience, for the road was efficiently blocked. No car could possibly pass, and turning back was out of the question. As the taxi slowed down, Father and the taxi driver debated as to what they should do. Before they realized it, however, they were surrounded on all sides and the car was forced to stop. Father prayed earnestly that their lives might be spared.

The mob seemed to have lost all their human traits. Immediately, they began their work of destruction, making so much noise that no one could be heard. The driver tried to protect my father by shielding him with his arms and shouting loudly, "This is a foreigner! Don't harm him; he is a foreigner!" But alas, no one could hear him. The mob went mad, swinging their clubs and shooting into the air. They rushed onto the running boards of the car and grabbed my father by the arms. A tug-of-war ensued, each side trying to pull him out of the car. Finally, one side succeeded. The others contented themselves with his suitcases, which they opened, strewing his belongings around on the road.

The men who held Father pushed and pulled him around, trying to place him in a position so that everyone could witness his execution. During all this brutal process, he could do nothing except pray, and pray he did, most earnestly, that the Lord's will would be done. At the moment the mob was ready for the execution, two men dressed in spotless white suits suddenly appeared and placed their hands over Father's head. As soon as these men appeared, a deathly silence settled on the crowd. Clubs, knives, and guns were lowered, and many threw their weapons away.

The two men in white, so different in appearance from the others in the crowd, with deep, stern voices commanded the sheepish mob to make way for the missionary. They lifted him by the arms and led him to the car, telling the mob to pick up his things and give them back to him, which they promptly did.

Then the two strangers ordered the driver to take the missionary back whence he had come and told my father that he was not to go home during the remainder of the revolution but stay by his work. They mounted the running boards, placed their arms across the car, and motioning the mob aside, told the driver to proceed. When they were well away from the mob, the two strangers disappeared. No one knew them or had ever seen them before, nor have they been seen since. Father's prayer had been answered, and many a time after this experience, he thanked and praised the Lord for his deliverance. ❧

*R*obert *T. Jack's story, published in a 1948* Youth's Instructor, *was set in Argentina. We learn some interesting things about angel behavior in the story: First, even when the person in danger tries to circumvent them, rather than giving up and leaving the obstinate person to his or her fate, the angels persist and make absolutely certain that the individual in question is saved from harm; second, angels often appear reluctant to show their faces (they are all business, not there to grandstand); third, they almost never remain when the danger is removed—they are not there to accept thanks; and fourth, they often reveal they know a great deal about the threatened person's personal life.*

OMNIPRESENCE

Robert T. Jack

Strange indeed, this stranger whose face remained in the shadows. No matter what he did to find out the identity of this sudden apparition on horseback, in the gloom, he was outsmarted every time. And why was he butting in when he had no right to do so? And how did the stranger know so much about him? It just made no sense.

"Giddap," called young Dan Billings to Meg, the black mare, as he spurred her along the darkened path. The sun had begun to go down behind the shoulder of the mountain, and he was hurrying homeward. The small city in Argentina where his wife and two-and-a-half-month-old baby were waiting for him was still more than twenty miles away.

As he rode, he thought of the business that had taken him to a neighboring town three days before, and of the dispute he had had with Señor Lopez and Señor Villa over the Holstein cow. At the thought of Señor Villa's angry face, Dan's heart pounded. The man had threatened his life, and he was the type of character who would stop at nothing to gain his end.

I'm getting jumpy; Villa was only momen-tarily angry. It must be the darkness and my long journey that are playing pranks on my nerves, Dan told himself. Nevertheless, it was consoling to remember his wife's parting words: "May God protect you!"

As he rode along, he had made up his mind to take the tortuous trail over the eastern hills. By this shortcut, the distance home would be only twelve miles. That would not be so bad. *I can make it tonight by ten-thirty,* he thought, and rode on at a slower pace while the sun slipped out of sight, leaving the twilight to wrestle with the oncoming night.

But it was lonely, and so he talked aloud to Meg about his duties as mayor of Trujillo, and of his decision that Señor Lopez, and not Señor Villa, owned the cow in question. He explained to the mare how the loss of the cow among the poor meant the loss of the family milk supply. But Meg gave no indication that she was listening, even when Dan went on to tell her of Señor Villa's menacing attitude, and how as a Christian he had disregarded the threat and looked to God for His protection.

While Mayor Billings was thus reviewing the recent events to Meg, a small voice, seemingly from within, kept telling him not chance the hill trail. *Go the longer way,* it seemed to urge. His thoughts and feelings were confused, but again he blamed this on his long journey and the eerie stillness of the deserted countryside.

A bouquet of nodding palms marked the beginning of the shortcut, a zigzagging trail which paralleled a brawling brook. "At last," sighed Dan, "only twelve miles more to go!" It was then nearly eight-twenty.

Suddenly, his horse whinnied and threw her head high in the air.

"Whoa! What's the matter with you, Meg?" he exclaimed impatiently. "Did you see a ghost or something?" At that moment, a rider appeared on a horse which looked as though it had been sculptured from fresh-fallen snow. Whether they had descended or ascended, Dan was not sure, but there they were standing before him.

Even in the shadowy twilight, he could see that the rider was a strong, handsomely built man. For a moment, there was not a sound. When Meg had been quieted, the figure spoke: "I see that you're taking this route over the hills. You're making a mistake, friend. It will be better if you go the other way."

Shaken by the rider's sudden appearance, Dan was slow to answer. He was vaguely conscious of how effortlessly the man handled his mount, and how well he kept his seat. "Who are you?" he asked suddenly. "What do you know of me?"

He was reasonably sure that the stranger was purposely reining his steed in such a way as to make it impossible for him to see anything but the back of his head or, at best, an unrevealing glimpse of his profile. And, furthermore, he was certain that this rider was not Señor Villa. For this Dan was thankful.

"I'm just a friend of yours," replied the man, and again he cautioned Dan to take the other route by pointing toward it while slowly riding off in the general direction of the hills.

Mayor Billings sat motionless on his horse, wondering what to do. Should he disregard this advice or turn and go the longer way home? The last few moments had been so packed with excitement that he had all but forgotten his wife and baby. Now again he was faced with the desire to reach them as quickly as possible.

"I'll retrace my steps a little way, and wait just long enough for this stranger to go on, then I'll return and continue over the hills," he decided.

A voice, certainly not his wife's, but seemingly from within, thundered in his ears, *"May God protect you!"*

But, stubbornly, Dan turned back for about six hundred yards, then he again headed for the hills. "What a strange person," mumbled Dan. *"Who* could he have been? What was his purpose in concerning himself about me?"

He could not answer his own questions. Even if he could have done so, he did not have time, for as suddenly and as mysteriously as the stranger had first appeared, he now reappeared, only a horse's length ahead.

There were no side roads from which the rider could have crossed the path. Where had he come from? This was just too weird! Dan sat on his horse like a man in a cast. His heart alternately stopped, beat, skipped, and raced, the more he thought about his strange companion.

"So you've decided to go over the hills after all?" the man challenged. Dan said nothing, for words refused to come to him. "I'm cautioning you *not* to travel the shortcut, even though I know that you're anxious to get home to your wife and baby."

How could this utter stranger possibly know about my wife and baby? questioned Dan to himself, and again he noted the rider's calm assuring voice, his broad shoulders, his expert reining in of his mount so that at no time could he get more than a fleeting glimpse of the side of his face.

"I'll ride along with you a while. Perhaps the time will seem to pass more quickly," the horseman offered laconically.

By now Dan was fully convinced that he should not continue along the shortcut. Considerable time had already passed, and he was aware of his own fatigue and that of his mare. The tortuous, uphill climb would probably be more strenuous than either he or Meg could take anyway. Then, too, by deciding now on the longer route, he could stay overnight at a friend's house, located about six miles down the road.

Dan knew that his wife would be disappointed at his failure to return that night; but, at the same time, he had not given her assurance that he would get back that evening but only that he would *try* to be back in three days, and this was the third day.

The stranger's offer to ride along was paradoxically comforting and perplexing. It was comforting to know that he would have someone to talk to, but perplexing because he still did not know who his companion was, or where he had come from. But he thanked him for his thoughtfulness and apparent interest.

Suddenly, he thought how he might get a

better look at the stranger's face. He would light a match so that he could see the time, and perhaps from the reflection, he could catch the glimpse he so much desired.

"Hold up just a second, I want to see the time," he suggested, trying to sound casual. Both horses whinnied and stopped. Dan lit his match, read the time aloud, "Nine-thirty-five," and glanced up at his companion.

But no sooner had he spoken the time than the match went out, and he could see no more of the rider's features than he had already observed.

Through the trees the moon made a patchwork of yellow streaks across the path, but even with this added light he still could not make out the features of his strange companion. Finally, Dan decided against asking the stranger why he was purposely concealing his identity. Maybe there would be opportunity to do so later. And as they approached his friend's home, he remarked, "It is not necessary for me to complete my journey tonight. I can stay here with my neighbor, and ride on home in the morning. I know that you will be welcome too."

With that he rode toward the house, where a light was visible within, and immediately dismounted, thinking that his strange friend would do the same. But he remained in his saddle.

Dan's mare took his attention for a moment while he unfastened the saddlebag, and when he looked up, the mysterious rider had vanished!

"Why, where are you? Sir! Sir! Sir!" cried Dan almost hysterically. There was no answer.

His friends, startled by his cries, came running from the house. The woman took Dan inside and bade him relax while her husband stabled Meg for the night. When they were all gathered in the living room, he told them of the uncanny appearance and disappearance of his rider companion.

Calling her husband aside, Mrs. Garcia whispered, "Dan is imagining things because he is so tired. I'll run upstairs and fix a bed for him, and you help him undress."

The next morning, the unexpected guest thanked his friends as he prepared to leave for the last lap of the journey home. He thought it best not to mention his experience to them again, for he knew they thought his imagination had been working overtime. When he reached home, his wife exclaimed, before he could say a word, "Thank God, you're safe, Dan! The police were out all night looking for Villa, and they found him at daybreak camped on the hill trail."

"But how did they know he was looking for me?"

"Lopez reported it after he and Villa had had another argument over the cow. During the argument, Villa told Lopez that he had been out lying in wait for you the night before and that he was going to get you last night for sure," Mrs. Billings explained.

Then Dan told his wife of his experiences of the previous evening, and together they walked to the baby's bed. There they dropped to their knees and thanked God for His marvelous protection and deliverance of one of His children. ❧

*T*he moment we agreed to write this book, first on our to-do list was to get my wife's sister, Marla, to write down the story we'd heard her and her husband, Gary, tell to us several times in the years since they returned to the United States after mission service in Africa. Getting someone to actually write out a story is, more often than not, most difficult. Reason being, it's far easier to tell a story than write it out. Since we had such a short time in which to complete this particular manuscript, we had to badger Marla. What a relief when it finally came, for we felt it must be part of this angel story collection. We're confident you'll agree.

We Should Have Been Dead

Marla Palmer Marsh

There they were: on the grass were positioned about twenty soldiers with submachine guns all pointed at them!
They had no Plan B to turn to—so what should they do?

"Hodi," called a young seminary student from the edge of the yard. "May I come in?" Quickly I answered him and invited him inside where it was cooler. After greeting me, Solomon asked if my husband would be willing to come to his family's island in Lake Victoria and have camp meeting for them. "We even have a place for your husband to land his airplane, and we will provide the food for you too. Please come!"

My husband made arrangements with a mission in Kenya, which was closer to the island than we were. A large group was going to join us for the weekend. They were going to come across the eighteen miles of open water in a large dugout canoe. This was going to be a wonderful event with good speakers and even a generator to run a sixteen millimeter projector and show a movie about improving one's health. Oh, yes. It was going to be a marvelous weekend!

On a Friday morning, we flew off in our small Super Cub plane. We flew about fifty miles northwest to the large town of Musoma, where we needed to obtain a visa from the immigration office. It was a mile or so to the office, and walking there and back took about one hour. It was a beautiful East African day, and we anticipated and chatted about how much fun we would have.

The airport official was very helpful, and we told him we would return Sunday around noon. "Oh, that's good," he said. We waved goodbye and boarded the little plane. Our two-year-old son Richie sat on my lap on the backseat. We both sat behind my husband. We bowed our heads and prayed for a pleasant and safe trip. Then we were off.

At a little grass airstrip about an hour's flight north into Kenya, we landed and taxied up to a little hut. It was at this point I was told that I would be waiting here until Gary came back from the island. "I'll go out with Solomon and then come back and get you." Just then I saw a man walking up the road, and he waved to us. It was Solomon.

Gary apologized to him for being late. Gary had planned to be there at 10:00 A.M., but since we had had to walk to the immigration office, it delayed us about an hour. So it was now 11:00 A.M. Solomon was not troubled at all, and in fact said that during the night he had had a dream which indicated to him that we would get there about 11:00 A.M., and he had just arrived. He hadn't waited at all. *Wow!* We thought. *That is special.*

Soon Gary and Solomon were on their way, and Richie and I sat down to wait. It was about a fifteen-minute flight out to the island, and Gary wanted to have a little time to check out the place where he was to land. Solomon had indicated it was an airport, but there was no indication of one on any flight map. As he approached the island, Gary noticed a wide horseshoe-shaped cliff. A pretty elementary school was nestled at the back of the circle. Across the opening was a large green field, and he flew low over it to check the ground for obstacles, holes, or livestock. It looked good and it was a good length for landing a Super Cub, except for an anthill about halfway down the field. There would be room if he made a dog-leg to avoid it. So he circled and landed.

But, my goodness, did he ever have to shut that engine down in a hurry! The people poured out from every hut in the area and from the school. Never before had a plane landed on the island, so they were excited, the women trilling their tongues with high-pitched squeals.

Gary and Solomon crawled out and the men helped them push the plane while the school children jumped and smiled and squealed and shook their hands, and stared at them in joy. It was a great day for the island. They had a little program ready too. They sang songs, and the headmaster welcomed them. He told them they would be staying in the schoolrooms. The students sang another song and gave a great shout in the direction of the cliff—then waited. Echoes ricocheted. They repeated it several times, and then Gary was free to fly back for us.

Soon we heard the hum of his little plane engine, and then we excitedly jumped in and took off. We flew to Kisumu and refueled before heading out to the island. When we landed, it was still big excitement for them, but they stood back and let the plane taxi up to the school this time. Then we all got out and talked with the people.

Right about then the big dugout canoe arrived on the shore. There were a lot of people and a lot of luggage to bring ashore. Many hands pitched in, and soon we were all together and comparing their trip with ours, settling in for the stay, and getting acquainted with each other.

Ladies soon arrived with large baskets heaped upon their heads. Loads of bananas, papayas, and pineapples. Quickly, fruit salad was made, and ugali (white corn meal mush), and several other tasty dishes too. Supper was wonderful.

Evening time came and we began to sing hymns and share the love of Jesus with them. Time flew. And soon it was time to go to bed. We all lay down and tried to sleep, but we found that our sleeping bags were meant more for a long winter's nap than for a night in the tropics at eighty degrees. We could stay under the cover only so long, and then out we came to cool off. But . . . when we came out from the covers, the mosquitoes were waiting for us.

It was a very long night. By morning, Richie had eighty-three bites on his face alone. We knew we all were in trouble. Malaria would be coming soon. In fact, we were going to get malaria at least twice. Oh, dear! We hadn't even remembered to bring a mosquito net. All of us discussed our condition; had any of us brought bug spray or nets? Could we share? None of us wanted to repeat the experience a second night. Some had spray, some had ointment, but no one had remembered a mosquito net. Saturday night was much better.

Sunday morning dawned soon and we were up and packed by eight. Another lovely meal—lots of good fruit—was served. I remember that the most. We took some pictures of the whole dugout group—all seventeen. Then we helped them get their gear down to the dugout. We bid them a pleasant journey and hurried to pack our things into the Super Cub. We planned to go to their mission first and get some good eggs from their chickens. The mission imported American hens and made it a business for the school. We had no such resource in our mission.

We left about 9:30 A.M. It took a thirty-minute flight to reach their mission. But since they had no airstrip, we buzzed the treasurer's house in Kisii. Don and Lois Folkenberg came out to the airstrip and then took Gary over to the mission so we could buy some eggs! Wow! When they returned thirty-five minutes later, they had a stack of those gray trays that hold two and a half dozen each.

Five layers. That is twelve and a half dozen eggs! Gary handed me the stack. I put Richie on my left knee and the eggs on my right knee. Then I called out to Lois, "If we go down, it's omelette!"

Well, we had to get going back to Musoma, the large immigration town, and get there around noon, as we had promised. We needed to check in with immigration and declare our twelve and a half dozen eggs as our only import. We had about one hour and we had an hour's flight to make. Things were working out really well. Right on time.

As we came alongside the Musoma runway, on "down wind," Gary noticed something a bit strange—different from the norm. I was not aware. I was enjoying the view and not thinking of any danger at all.

At this airport, there was a little garage against the outside fence and about midway down the runway. The airport personnel would generally get the little pickup fire truck out and race to the end of the runway where you touch down. Then they would stay right alongside your plane all the way to the parking apron. But they didn't even move their truck this time. Gary noticed.

We landed, then taxied until coming alongside the parking lot. Between the parking lot and the runway was a twenty-foot-wide strip of grass. I was shocked as I looked out the window. On the grass were positioned about twenty soldiers with submachine guns all aimed at us! I tapped Gary on the back and yelled, "Do you see what I see?" Gary only nodded his head Yes.

Now what? What was the reason for this? We were full of questions. But we have found that if you get too dramatic, it does you no good. You calmly deal with the situation and pray for wisdom. As Gary swung the tail around and parked parallel to the strip of grass in the same direction as we landed, he let the engine slow, then die down. When he swung the upper part of the door up and latched it, the sergeant in command came up to the plane and asked Gary to come with him. They walked across the parking apron and stood on the sidewalk that led to the airport offices. The airport manager was there to welcome us but was repulsed by the soldiers. They refused to listen to him. He told them that he was expecting us but was sent away.

Then the sergeant began to question Gary: "Who are you?" "Where do you live?" "How long have you lived there?" "What do you do there?" "What do you teach?" "Are you the headmaster?" "Are you the only white man there?" "Is this your family?" "Do you have more children than this?" "Did you know that the airport was closed?" "Where have you been?" "Where are you coming from?" On and on he went. Then he began to repeat the same questions.

Gary could see this line of questions was leading nowhere, so he asked the sergeant, "Do you know the Regional Police Officer?" The sergeant stared back at Gary—hardly believing the question. "Yes, do you know him too?"

Gary declared that he did know him: "If you will go get him, he will tell you who I am." So the sergeant sent a soldier to bring the Regional Police Officer to the airport. In the meantime, he and Gary walked back over to the airplane where Rich and I were waiting. Gary leaned into the window and requested that we come with them. So I lifted the eggs off my knee and handed them to Gary. While Rich stayed on the seat, I climbed out of the plane and then turned around and picked him up. The eggs were returned to the seat of the plane, and we all walked across the parking apron together. It seemed a strange walk to me. I didn't know what was going on. We stopped at the end of the sidewalk again and waited—for what? I didn't know what. By this time there were several soldiers off to my right standing, sitting on the cement barrier, or kneeling on the grass. They were silent, the sergeant was silent, and we just waited.

Shortly, the little gray Jeep came back and out jumped the Regional Police Officer, who walked quickly over to the sergeant. They conversed quietly for a moment, and then the Regional Police Officer turned and came over to Gary and greeted him, *"Habari, Bwana Marshi?"* ("How are you?") Gary replied and then explained what was going on. Then the police officer turned and spoke with the sergeant again.

This time when the Regional Police Officer returned to us, he just shook his head in amazement. It seems that while we were away that weekend, the army had decided to take control of the airport and closed it. They had orders to shoot all aircraft that came to land at the airport. All the soldiers were on the grass with their guns trained on us and had tried to shoot us—but not one of them could make their guns fire! He pointed over to the soldiers and said something to them, and they opened the clips and many bullets spilled out onto the ground. We watched dumbfounded as we began to realize how close we'd come to death.

The Regional Police Officer confessed to Gary that he could not understand why they had not been able to shoot—but we were free to go home.

We quietly turned and began to walk back to the plane. We didn't say anything, being in a state of shock. We shuffled eggs as Richie and I climbed back in. Gary climbed into the front seat. Believe me, he didn't take very long to get the plane started and moving! He then did something that is not usually done! He headed the nose of the plane downwind away from the soldiers and the guns, pouring the coals on and giving the little plane all the power he could muster. As we began to lift off the ground, I heard a normally very quiet man in the front seat begin to sing in a shaky voice, "All night, all day, angels watching over me, my Lord. All night, all day . . ." We were headed home.

Postscript:

The next day, the Head Ranger of the Serengeti National Park had his plane shot at. Then the following day, the East African Airlines had one of their regularly scheduled planes shot at and hit. Both planes diverted and no one was hurt. Our little plane, with nothing but a cloth skin, had been the first plane to land on that very first day of closure. Clearly, had God's angels not been watching over us, we'd never be writing this story! ❧

SECTION FIVE

That's right—he rescues you from hidden traps, shields you from deadly hazards.
Psalm 91:3 (*The Message*)

*S*ome years ago, this story was sent to me by Marilyn Nelson of Walla Walla, Washington. She is the most indefatigable story searcher I know. Faithfully, over the years, she has sent us batch after batch of her favorite stories. Of this one's origin, she discovered that George Plume, at the time he wrote this story, was a freelance writer living in Union Gap, Washington. However, when she attempted to discover whether he still resided there, apparently he'd moved on. No one knows where. Nor its origins—the copy sent me had been mimeographed.

THE SEA ON MY BACK

George Plume

But he didn't want to die! Yet that was what was happening to the young submariner as the sub dove to escape the Japanese patrol bomber. But would George Plume die? For he'd been locked out of the sub as the ship dove.
Was there any hope for him?

Every submariner lives with one terrifying fear: in a life-or-death situation, he might have to shut the hatch or close a watertight door on shipmates, thus abandoning them to death—or even suffer the same fate himself. It is something you accept and never think about.

Certainly, I wasn't thinking about it as the USS *Harder* surged smoothly through the Pacific off the coast of Japan that night in 1944. It was a routine evening on war patrol.

Yet, after almost twenty years, I can still see that night, hear it, feel it . . . even smell it.

It was the night I knew there was a God: the night I experienced His real power and felt the indescribable wonder of His presence.

We were slipping along at ten knots, using the hours of darkness to recharge our batteries and air banks while patrolling on the surface.

Lieutenant Sam Logan was the Officer of the Day on the bridge, a lanky whiz of a submarine officer. The second section had relieved the watch at 2000 hours (8:00 P.M.) And I had taken over as quartermaster on watch.

The lookouts changed at staggered intervals, to prevent clogging the hatchway in the event the bridge watch had to come scrambling down. There was a man coming and going every half hour. Up through the control room hatch, turn, two steps over to the bridge ladder and up, using the dog wheel on the open hatch cover as a handle to pull themselves through the manhole.

On diving, the last man off deck yanks a lanyard which brings the cover slamming down. The quartermaster must then reach up and swiftly spin the dog wheel to extend the dog levers under the hatch rim into locking position.

Except for scattered rain squalls, visibility was good that night. With the enemy coast only an hour's flying time away, our lookouts were "keeping their binoculars warm."

I had just come back down into the conning tower after a topside look around when a low-flying Japanese patrol bomber burst out of a rain squall directly behind us, roaring in for the kill.

The after-lookout screamed the warning, "Clear the bridge!"

The three lookouts came tumbling down the hatch. As quartermaster on duty, I leaped for the forward corner to be ready to help Logan secure the cover.

Dive—Dive! bellowed through the speakers. Down came Logan, lanyard in first, pulling the hatch cover closed.

"He's right on top of us!" Logan panted.

Then he swiveled his head and shouted to the control room, "Take her deep . . . FAST!"

With the trip latch apparently engaged, Logan spun away to jump down the control room ladder and take over the dive. There wasn't time to wait for a "green board" signal below, which would signify all hull openings closed. Thirty seconds from the diving alarm, our decks had plunged beneath the surface.

In those thirty seconds, my surprise at the suddenness of the bomber attack turned to utter shock as water poured down upon me from the partially closed hatch. It was stuck and would not close.

I gripped the wheel desperately, twisting back and forth with all my strength, but it was immovable. Fighting water that all but blinded me, I looked over my left shoulder frantically. The helmsman had gone below, right behind Lieutenant Logan. I was alone.

There was a wild shout from below, "We still got a red light on the bridge hatch!"

But I couldn't answer. The descending water was a fierce torrent, and I was choking as I kept up my maddened twisting and jerking at the dog wheel. Roaring in my ears, the terrible noise of the in-rushing sea increased.

A thunderous explosion sledge-hammered the hull, then another, causing the *Harder* to jump convulsively. The submarine lurched sideways under the smashing blow of a third Japanese depth charge.

Then, over all the terrifying noise, I heard a heavy clang as the control room hatch slammed shut below. They had abandoned me!

Surfacing, to stop the uncontrollable flooding and save me, meant destruction for the *Harder* and death for every man on board. But I didn't think of that. I didn't think of anything. I tried to scream for help. And then I went berserk as I wrenched and tore at that jammed dog wheel. All I knew was that I didn't want to die—not alone in here—like this. The awful force above tore me away from the hatch mechanism, while slowly from below, the water rose in that tiny, steel cubicle. I grabbed for the ladder.

I was paralyzed by fear beyond description, a miserable fright born of complete helplessness. Yet, deep within me was the recurring thought: *God, help me! God, help me!* It was not an uttered or conscious prayer. My panic had carried me past such awareness. I couldn't ask for God's intervention.

And that is when it happened.

Suddenly, through the chaos, there came a quieting and a strange feeling of reassurance. It seemed, inexplicably, that in the few moments I had left, there was plenty of time. Then from the calm within me came these words which I shall hear for the rest of my days, *"George, open the hatch!"*

Without question or thought, obediently, and with what strength that had left my body, I reached up. This time I turned the dog wheel back, to open the hatch. The dogs stuck for a heartbeat then slid back, easily . . . and the monstrous sea pressure immediately pressed the hatch tight on the rim! Instantly, the crushing downpour dwindled to a trickle.

Methodically, I slowly reversed the wheel and secured the hatch. The trickle stopped. I turned to look about me in wonder. Then I forged through the water to get my hand on the speaker "talk" lever and said, "It's OK. The hatch is closed. You can pump this place out now."

I've marveled for years, in thinking back, that even then, without conscious thought I did not say, "I closed the hatch." The truth bespoke itself. *The hatch was closed, but not by me.*

The conning tower was pumped out, the hatch below opened, and I climbed down to rejoin my back-pounding, joyful shipmates. Commander Sam Dealey, one of the finest men I shall ever know, had quiet words of commendation as the boat cruised safely in the depths.

But through all of it there was that one question . . . that single, small, lingering doubt. I turned to Lieutenant Logan and asked, "Did anybody down here use the speaker to tell me to open the hatch?" The looks of surprise around the control room told me what I guess I already knew. *Someone else had helped me.*

Today, almost twenty years later, I still feel the mighty power of that reassurance—that He is a practical, physical, ever-present God, that He has a plan for each of us. And in that knowledge I have a serene, indestructible, immovable faith which I, simply, humbly, and gratefully, try to share with those about me.

George Plume received the Silver Star for heroic action during World War II. Since his discharge from the navy, he worked as a Honolulu police officer, a newspaper reporter, a radio announcer, and a freelance writer. ❦

*F*ew of us have such deep, never-failing, absolute trust in God as that revealed in this 1931 Youth's Instructor *story. As mentioned in my dedication, one of the only such individuals I have ever known was my father. He was so confident of his relationship with God that he would not have hesitated for an instant to call on Him for legions of angels were he in need of them for the work of the church.*

Force felt, or sensed, but not seen: such angel stories send chills up our spines. You know mighty angels are at work and natural law is being turned on its head—you just can't see them.

FAITH

Mildred Hatch

Uncle Perry wasn't worried. His sleds were the very best to be had, and his equipment was in perfect order. Steel-pointed brake points and a strong brake pole—what could possibly go wrong? He was soon to find out!

Uncle Perry had learned to love his Creator and all of His created beings, and in his simple, childlike love and faith in God, seemed to enjoy a close communion with the heavenly Father denied to most men. His confidence in his heavenly Father was utter; his faith in His guidance and constant care, absolute. It was not surprising, then, that trust and confidence had driven all fear from his heart, nor that strange happenings sometimes broke the monotony of his rather strenuous and lonely bachelor life.

Uncle Perry made his principal living by cutting and hauling wood from his ranch to Trail, the British Columbia town below. There he sold it in large quantities to the smelter. As the ranch was on a high flat above the town which lies in the canyon of the Columbia River, the road led down a long, steep grade along the canyon wall.

It was midwinter. The warmth of the river below kept the snow which fell melting continuously, and the ice formed during the cold nights made the "big grade" treacherous at its best. One day Uncle Perry was delivering an order of two cords of heavy tamarack wood. The trail was treacherous and slippery, but the undertaking held no terrors for him. Had he not made the trip many times? His sleds were the very best to be had, and his equipment was in perfect order. For this kind of work on icy hills, a very effective brake is provided in the form of a pair of heavy steel points which work on each side of the sled runners and are forced by lever action into the hardest ice and snow. Thus the sled may be stayed quite safely. The leverage is applied by means of a brake pole attached to the rear sled bunks and controlled from the driver's seat by means of a strong rope running through pulley blocks.

As Uncle Perry and Pete (one of the farm-hands) reached the brow of the hill that memorable morning, the older man stopped his team, a heavy pair of fiery colts, and proceeded to look the load over for safety's sake. All was well. As he took up his reins again, he bowed his head for just a moment. Uncle Perry never failed to seek the assurance of protection from above when a situation looked dangerous. Then he trusted his Father implicitly.

The team moved over the top. The downgrade was a glare of ice. It took all the holding power of their sharp, steel-shod feet to keep them standing. They seemed to sense the danger and moved nervously ahead of the loaded sled, while the brake teeth dug deeper, ever deeper, into the slippery surface as the rope was drawn tighter, and still tighter.

Suddenly, a quarter of the way down, the brake pole broke! The heavy load plunged forward against the horses. Startled, they leaped ahead, only to be checked by the stern pressure on their bits. But the load was too heavy. Their feet were slipping! Thoroughly frightened, they began to rear and plunge. Just then the sled tongue broke!

Pete will never forget that moment—the dizzy sloughing of the sled toward the brink, those fear-maddened horses! He looked at Uncle Perry, who was still holding the reins calmly in his hands. Realizing a dire necessity, he had turned his face heavenward, toward his ever-present Help which had never failed him. His lips moved—just a single sentence. Pete wondered what he had prayed.

Then, as the boy's eyes fell once more into the canyon below, he observed an Italian workman splitting wood in his backyard. A new terror seized him. What if the load should fall over on the man? He tried to cry out to him, but his throat was tight with fear, and no sound came. He tried again. His voice was strange to himself. There was a pause. Then something happened ahead!

It was as if someone had seized those maddened horses by their bridles, and was forcing them backward against the load. Pete saw their heads go up, saw them struggle to free their heads from that hold! They were forced into a sitting position so that the sled gouged into their flesh deep enough to drive any team crazy, and still they remained in that cruelly strained position. Then it dawned upon the young man that Someone really *was* holding the team. Someone very strong. God had sent help! The lines in Uncle Perry's hands were loosened, and he said quietly, "Let's get the load off."

Soon there were many volunteer helpers to assist in the work of unloading the sled; and as the men worked, their eyes turned ever and again in wonderment mixed with fear to those young horses holding that strained, unnatural position. Bodily the sled was dragged back to safety; and the horses, released, gained their footing, snorting and foaming. They were soothed and quieted as Uncle Perry patted their noses.

In that rough, ungodly company of men who assisted in the emergency, there was not one who did not solemnly remove his hat, realizing that he was in the presence of divine power. ❧

*U*nfortunately, the only copy of this story I've ever found has no identification as to source. Judging by the type and formatting, I'm guessing it is a Youth's Instructor *story.*

It almost seems a norm among angel or voice stories, that when a divine command is given, each repetition is stronger and more intense than the one before, and the third almost invariably is all but irresistible, just as is true in this story.

Only in this case, uncharacteristically where angel stories are concerned, there is no inkling or referring to a Higher Power. But the angelic voice is there, to save everyone on the ship.

STOP THE SHIP!

W. S. Chapman

Why was it that the ship's first mate felt impelled to do something not only uncharacteristic but could also cost him his job?
It just didn't make sense!

A very remarkable story is told by a captain of a passenger steamer and is vouched for by the editor of the *Hiemlands Postn,* a prominent Norwegian paper published at Horten, Norway.

At the time mentioned, the narrator was first mate on a large Norwegian passenger steamer. The voyage had been prosperous and pleasant, and up to a certain morning nothing of an unusual character had taken place. The second mate had charge of the deck, it being the captain's watch, when, at the dog-watch, at 2:00 A.M., the first mate turned out to relieve him.

As he came on deck, the chill air caused him to shiver and exclaim, "Why, how cold it is!"

"No, it's not cold. You have just come from a warm cabin and feel the chill."

"Possibly that's so, but it seems to me it's very cold."

After the second mate had gone below, the first mate paced the deck slowly, as officers on watch are accustomed to do. As he did so, a peculiar tenderness of feeling stole over him. Visions of home, the wife and children, came to his mind. What if he should never see them, or home, again?

The thought stirred and chilled him. He stopped nervously, but resumed his walk as the cold struck him more forcibly. Once more the subdued feeling crept over him, thoughts of home returned, and mentally he again asked himself the question, *What if I should never see them, or home, again?* Suddenly, and as naturally as though someone stood beside him and were talking, he heard the command, *"Stop the ship!"*

Startled, he peered about him into the darkness, but no one was near. Bewildered and half ashamed of himself, for sailors are often accused of being superstitious and this man had no foolishness in his makeup, he resumed his walk, only to have the same tender feelings again take possession of him. This time he thought not only of his family and home but of the hundreds of sleeping passengers below whose safety rested in his hands and who depended upon his faithfulness and vigilance. *What,* he thought, *if none of these should ever see their homes again?*

Hardly had the thought been born than he heard the voice call for the second time, and in a more imperative manner, *"Stop the ship!"* At once he turned to the wheelhouse, for he was on the bridge, and passed back to telegraph to the engineer to slow down—but hesitated. It was an unpardonable offense to stop a steamer at sea without a just cause, and what excuse could he use with the captain should he do so?

In perplexity, he hailed the lookout at the bow—"Is all well there?"

"All well here, sir," came the answer.

So he tried to shake off the feeling of dread that was slowly possessing him, buttoned his coat more closely, and resumed his walk, shivering now more from nervousness than the cold.

But again the voice halted him, clearer and more decisive: *"Stop the ship!"*

Hesitating no longer, the mate flashed the signal to the engineer to slow down, and as the vibrations from the propellers ceased, the alarmed passengers, with the captain at their head, came up on the deck, asking what was the trouble.

An inspiration seemed to seize the mate. In a tone that forbade dispute, he ordered the helmsman to put the ship hard aport and took hold of the wheel to help hurry the act, then sprang to the rear and signaled for full speed. The great ship responded with a quiver, and her bow turned off as she slowly forged ahead and away from her course, just as a huge leviathan of an iceberg grazed her bow, dipping and rising with the rolling sea that dashed in fury at its sides, and slid past like a black, gaunt demon roaring in anger at the loss of its prey. ❧

*T*his Youth's Instructor *story of the 1930s is unusual in that it is written from the vantage point of a child; consequently, children ought to love having it read out loud to them. Several of the stories in this collection make spiritual music integral parts of their story plots; this is certainly true with the role that "God Will Take Care of You" plays in the narrative.*

GOD WILL TAKE CARE OF YOU

J. Echo Cossentine

What was that rushing sound? It didn't take long to find out! The house was flooded, the water was rapidly rising, Mother was gone. What should the twins do?

Jearld and Jessie, the two black-eyed, curly-haired twins who lived in the small farmhouse by the big dam, were almost twelve. They loved fishing in the stream which wound its way through the garden behind the house. Jessie especially liked the little brook, for she could talk to it and it seemed to understand; at least its gentle murmur made her forget her childish troubles. Jearld had loosened the earth on the bank, and together they had planted flower seeds and watched eagerly as the tiny plants peeped through the dark, rich soil. And now the beautiful flowers were their reward. Sometimes Mother packed them a basket lunch, which they ate in the garden while they listened to the *buzz-z-z* of the bees as they flew from flower to flower, and the slight splash that came now and then as a frog leaped into the water.

But not all the twins' time was spent in play; they had to work, for their father had been laid to rest several years before, and their mother had been left with only the little farm by which to support herself and the children. Fortunately, Mrs. Johnson had had some experience in nursing, and by helping her neighbors, she was able to earn a little extra with which to buy food and clothing. The twins were a great help to her, and when she was away on a case, they would milk the cows, feed the chickens, and bring in the wood as faithfully as if she were there to watch them.

One warm spring day while they were eating their dinner, a neighbor drove up to the house and asked Mrs. Johnson to come quickly, for his wife was dying. Mother gave a few last-minute instructions to the children and reminded them to do their chores early and go to bed before it grew dark, so that they would not have to light a lamp. With this she was gone, and the twins were alone.

After they had finished their meal of bread

and milk, Jessie put the little kitchen in order, and then the two went to their garden by the brook. Together they played games and skipped stones, and when this became tiresome, they slipped off their shoes and stockings and waded in the fresh, cool water. But all too soon they noticed that the sun was sinking low in the west and that their shadows were fast growing longer. So they said goodbye to the quiet little stream— not realizing that it would be the last time—and hand in hand started on the path after the cows.

It did not take long to find them, and soon the cattle were back in the pasture, the hens fed, and the eggs gathered. Then just as the sun was saying good night to the world as it waved its beautiful rays of purple, red, and gold across the western sky, the twins started for the house.

It will soon be dark, they thought, and they hurried to prepare the evening meal. In almost no time the two were seated at the table and were thanking God for food and a home.

It was almost dark by the time the children started up the winding stairs to their rooms. After the prayers and good nights had been said, each jumped into bed and pulled the covers close, for, although it was spring, the evenings were still quite cool.

All was quiet; there was nothing to break the stillness except the noise of the crickets and now and then a hoot owl calling for his mate. Jearld and Jessie had played hard, and soon the sound of deep breathing told that each tired little twin was in dreamland.

Suddenly, Jearld awoke, *What is that strange sound I hear?* he murmured almost out loud, as he sat up in bed, rubbing his sleepy eyes. "Could it be?" Yes, it sounded like— "Sister," he called, running to her room across the hall, "Sister, wake up!" Sleepy Jessie rolled over, unmindful of her twin's pleading voice. "Sister!" Jearld shouted again, "Something is wrong; wake up quick!" At this Jessie was wide awake, and she, too, felt a queer sensation of fear creep through her, but she did not know why.

"What is it, Jearld? What is that rushing sound?"

"I don't know, Sis, but let's find out," he suggested. And together they went to the window and peered out into the black night. There was not a star in sight; in fact, it was so dark they could not even see the woodshed by the house. All they could hear was that awful rushing sound; it sounded like—water! *Could it be?* they thought.

"Jessie, you stay here," commanded Jearld in a tone which sounded like that of a real man; "I am going downstairs to find out what's the trouble, and don't you be afraid, for I'll take care of you."

When he reached the kitchen, he found the floor covered with water, but, pulling up his pajama legs, he waded through it and in the darkness succeeded in finding the lamp, which his mother always kept on the shelf, and lit it. This done, he started for the back door to find out where the water was coming from. But he had scarcely turned the doorknob when the door burst open and in rushed a wall of water. Flinging all the strength of his twelve-year-old body against the big door, he tried to shut it, but in vain; more water poured in, and it was getting deeper and deeper. Fear crept through his heart as he realized that it must be a flood and that they were in grave danger.

Upstairs Jessie was patiently waiting for her brother's return, and although she had faith that he would do all that he could, she was more than a little uneasy. In a short time, Jearld returned with a pale face, carrying the lamp in his hand.

"It's really bad, Jessie; I think we had better pray," he suggested. "You know our memory verse for last week said, 'The angel of the Lord encampeth round about them that fear him, and delivereth them,' and we need angels to protect us right now; so let's ask God to send them." Together the two knelt and asked their heavenly Father to keep them safe and also to be with their dear mother and keep her from harm.

Soon the water had risen to the second floor, and the twins were forced to seek safety in the attic, but as they were climbing up the attic stairs, their lamp went out, and as they had nothing with which to light it, they must remain in darkness.

Jessie was a bit fearful and might have cried had not her brother reminded her of God's promise, and added bravely, "God means what He says; so don't be afraid, Sister. Come, we will go to the window and sing, and perhaps we will feel better."

At one of the houses in that little country village several miles away, word was received that the big dam had broken, and men with boats were sent to rescue the poor, frightened people.

"It's a dark night, and we are going to have a hard time finding the houses and the people," said Mr. Smith, as the boat moved along in the darkness. "The water is already to the top of this house. But what is that I heard? Listen." And above the sound of rushing water came the sound of children's voices singing "God Will Take Care of You." "Tom, turn the boat around; there is a house back there. We went past it and didn't even see it." And as they listened, they found the origin of the hymns, and found the twins safe and unafraid.

One of the other boats rescued Mrs. Johnson, and in a few hours the twins were in their mother's arms. It was a happy time for the mother, for although her home was gone, she had her children and all were safe.

Jearld and Jessie will never forget that early spring night when they prayed for God to send His angels—and He really did! ❧

*B*oth the son and grandson of this remarkable story have vouched for its authenticity. None of the descendants were permitted to forget the angel that rode the rails that never-to-be-forgotten night.

And we can thus be certain that the same God who sent His angel to save the lives of all those riding on PG-16 will respond to each of us when we call—or even, perhaps, when we don't have time to.

In this story, we see through the engineer's eyes a well-dressed angel wearing a light gray suit and a soft fedora hat. He had a light-brown mustache, and his eyes were alight with wonderment. Most exceptional of all: even though he was standing outside the engine cab, and the train was traveling at full speed, the hat remained on the angel's head without being held or tying it in any way, and his clothes were not blown by the wind!

The Mysterious Rider on PG-16

Merton Henry Jr.

The Buffalo Flyer, *PG-16, was racing along a familiar stretch of train tracks, when the engineer saw him.*
Where did he come from!

The moon over the mountains of eastern Pennsylvania had turned the shining steel rails into two endless ribbons of silver that faded away into the night. *The Buffalo Flyer,* PG-16, winding its way along the valley route from Williamsport, rolled into the station at Sunbury on time.

There was a ten-minute layover there. That was where the crew of the Sunbury division took the train. And that was where William "Bill" Henry took the throttle.

The *Flyer* left Sunbury on schedule and was soon lost in the night, pounding the rails, winding up the river, keeping its appointment with the clock. The next station stop was Scranton, about eighty miles northeast in the mountains, up and beyond the valley of the Susquehanna River. Between Sunbury and Scranton was a stop where steam loco-motives refilled their water tanks. That water stop was called Port.

The crewmen worked well together. They had traveled the same familiar run day after day, night after night. As they traveled along—the engineer with his hand on the throttle and his eye on the rail, the fireman feeding coal into the hungry firebox, the flagmen with their signals—each was pretty much alone with his thoughts. No one knows what each crewman was thinking that night. No one knows the thoughts of Bill Henry as the train sped along the mountain railway. But Bill was a God-fearing man, a man whose character and integrity were above question.

Soon the night express was at Port, and water was dumped into the tanks. Again on schedule, with a blast of the whistle and in a cloud of black coal smoke, the train followed the steel pathway into the night.

Bill had his hand on the throttle, and Hank, his fireman, was shoveling coal into the roaring fire. The PG-16 was racing along the familiar course, each crewman absorbed in his own thoughts, when the engineer saw him!

They were just above Shickshinny, where the mining region began. There, in the dying light of a fading moon, Bill saw a man walk calmly up from the pilot in front of the locomotive and swing confidently up onto the steam chest. His back was to the cab and to the engineer. With his left hand he was holding onto the handrail, and with his right hand he gave a signal. He was well dressed, wearing a light-gray suit and a soft fedora hat. And he was continually giving the caution-stop signal.

Bill called to his fireman. "Hank, it looks as if we have a passenger!"

Hank came over and looked ahead. He, too, saw the rider. He looked at him for just a moment and then went back to his shovel. "Must be a bum that got on at Port."

As Bill watched, the man in gray stepped up onto the running board that led from the front of the engine back to the cab and gave another signal—*danger*—*stop*! Then he turned and for the first time looked at the engineer—the first time that Bill had seen his face.

Bill saw him clearly. He had a light-brown mustache, and his eyes bore an expression of wonderment. The train was still traveling at full speed, but the hat remained on the man's head without aid and his clothes were not blown by the wind. They remained in place just as if he were standing in his own parlor.

Then he changed his signal once more. This time, having walked a little closer to the cab, he gave the sign for an emergency stop!

Bill released the throttle, put on all brakes, and whistled for the flag. The PG-16 ground to a hard stop and the flagman went out, the first flagman ahead for two hundred feet and the second flagman back for three hundred feet to warn any other train that there was a halted locomotive on the tracks.

The first flagman had gone only about 150 feet when he signaled with his lantern. "Cave in!"

When the crew rushed ahead, they found only a gaping hole where there had been the twin rails and a tool shed.

The engineer and the fireman turned to inquire of the man in gray. But the mysterious night rider on that train was never found. He was never heard of again. He had disappeared just as mysteriously as he had appeared.

Bill Henry was a quiet, devoted Christian gentleman, and he didn't talk much to most people about the experience. When he did tell it, he left it to the hearer to identify the man in gray. But of one thing he was personally sure: that night he had a messenger from heaven riding his train. ❧

I unearthed the text of this story in the pages of an 1876 issue of *Frank Leslie's* Popular Monthly. *There is a direct lateral relationship between this story and my "Hanging On by the Fingers" in section one. Even though there's almost half a millennium between the two stories, the common denominators are similar, involving as they both do youth who feel invincible in their own strength, youth who dare to take foolish risks, youth who strike out on their own without human support systems, youth who are climbing mountain walls and get stuck, unable to move up, down, or sideways; youth who learn a great lesson from their hubris—and only God brings them through alive.*

MAXIMILIAN'S WISH

Author Unknown

The young emperor, thanks to a hubristic impulse, was now stranded on a high alpine wall, with no way to climb up, climb down, or climb out.
So what could he do to save himself?

Maximilian I, emperor of Germany, sometmes called the "Last Knight" from his chivalrous character, was in his youth remarkable for a high courage and love of adventure, which at times, led him to feats of rash daring.

Among the many lands over which he ruled, none was so dear to him as the mountainous Tyrol. Partly from the simple and loving loyalty of the hardy race of shepherds and the mountaineers who dwelt there, partly also because hunting among the Tyrolese Alps was one of his chief pleasures.

On Easter Monday, in the year 1493, the young emperor, who was staying in the neighborhood of Innsbruck, rose before dawn for a day's chamois-hunting. He took with him a few courtiers and some experienced hunters.

At sunrise they were already high up on the mountain pastures, which are the favorite haunts of the chamois; the valleys beneath them were still covered by a sea of white mist, while the golden rays of morning shone from an unclouded sky on the snowy peaks and ridges above them.

Maximilian fixed a longing gaze on the rocky summits, which stood out clear and sharp against the blue heavens. He felt the power of the fresh mountain air and the sublime scenery, and it filled him with the spirit of enterprise and daring.

"I wish," said he, "that I could gain today some spot which the foot of man has never trod before, and where no man should be able to follow; a spot amid the homes of the chamois and the eagle; where the busy hum of men should be lost to my ear, and all the crowded earth should lie beneath my feet; where even the thunderclouds should mutter far below me, while I stood in eternal sunshine! That would be a fit spot for the throne of an emperor!"

The courtiers replied that his majesty had but to wish and it would be fulfilled—to such a renowned hunter and intrepid mountaineer what could be impossible?

At this moment one of the huntsmen gave notice that he had sighted some chamois; the whole party, guided by him, cautiously approached a rocky point, behind which the animals were grazing. On this point of rock stood a single chamois, its graceful head raised, as if on the watch. Long before they were within shot range, they heard it utter the peculiar piping cry by which the chamois gives notice of danger to its fellows, and then off it bounded with flying leaps toward the rocky solitudes above. Maximilian followed on its track and had soon distanced his attendants.

To be a good chamois hunter, a firm foot and a steady head are required, for these beautiful little animals lead their pursuer into their own peculiar domain, the rocky wastes just below the regions of perpetual snow, and there they climb and spring with wonderful agility, and if they cannot escape, it is said that they will rather leap over a precipice and be dashed to pieces, than fall into the power of man.

Maximilian had all the qualities necessary for this adventurous chase and was generally most successful in it. Now he reached the brink of a chasm, which the chamois had passed; black yawned the abyss at his feet, while beyond the rocks rose steep and forbidding, with but one little spot where a man could find footing. One moment he paused, then with a light spring he gained the other side, while a shout, half of admiration, half of terror, burst from his astonished suite.

"That was a royal leap! Who follows?" cried Maximilian, with an exulting laugh. Then he sped onward, intensely enjoying the excitement of the chase.

For a moment he lost the chamois from view, and then it appeared again, its form standing out against the sky, on one of those rocky ridges that have been compared to the backbone of a fish, but are perhaps more like the upper edge of a steep gabled roof.

To gain this ridge it was needful to climb an almost perpendicular precipice; but Maximilian, nothing daunted, followed on, driving small iron holdfasts into the rock in places where he could gain no footing, and holding on by the hook, at the upper end of his iron-pointed Alpstick. At last he seized a projecting piece of rock with his hand, hoping to swing himself up by it, but the stone did not bear his weight; it loosened and fell, and the emperor fell with it.

Breathless and stunned, it was some minutes before he recovered consciousness after the fall. When he came to himself, he found that he had received no injury, except a few bruises, and his first thought was that he was most lucky to have escaped so well. Then he began to look about him. He had fallen into a sort of crevice, or hollow in the rocks; on one side there rose above him a high wall which it was impossible to scale; on the other they were hardly higher than his head, so that on this side he had no difficulty in getting out of the hollow.

Lucky again, thought Maximilian; but as he emerged from the crevice and rose from his feet, he remained motionless in awestruck consternation. He stood on a narrow ledge, a space hardly wide enough for two men abreast, and beneath him, sheer down to a depth of many hundred feet, sank a perpendicular wall of rock. He knew the place; it was called Saint Martin's Wall, from the neighboring chapel of Saint Martin; and the valley below it, which was now concealed from his view by white rolling clouds, was the Valley of Zierlein.

Above him rose the "wall," so straight and smooth that it was utterly hopeless to think of scaling it. The only spot within sight where a man could find footing was the narrow shelf on which he stood. The ledge itself extended but a few feet on either side and then ceased abruptly.

In vain Maximilian gazed round for some way of escape.

No handsbreadth was there to which to cling; no hold for foot or hand of the most expert climber—beneath, a sea of cloud; above, a sea of air.

Suddenly, he was startled by a whir and a rush of great wings in his face—it was a mountain eagle which swooped past him, and the wind of whose flight was so strong that it had nearly thrown him off his balance. He recollected that he had heard how these eagles try to drive any larger prey, too heavy to be seized in their talons, to the edge of a precipice, and so, by suddenly whirling round it, they may dash it over the brink; and how they had tried this maneuver more than once on hunters whom they found in critical and helpless positions.

And then his wish of the morning occurred to him. How literally and exactly it had been fulfilled! And how little could the emperor exult in his lofty and airy throne! He merely felt with a shudder his own exceeding littleness in the face of the great realities of nature and nature's God.

Beneath, in the valley of Zierlein, a shepherd was watching his flocks. As the sun rose higher and drew the mists off which clung round the foot of Saint Martin's Wall, he noticed a dark speck moving on the face of the rock. He observed it narrowly.

"It is a man!" he cried. "What witchcraft has brought him there?"

And he ran to tell the wonder to the inhabitants of the valley. Soon a little crowd collected and stood gazing up at Saint Martin's Wall.

"God be with him!" was the compassionate

exclamation of all. "He can never leave that spot alive—he must perish miserably of hunger!"

Just then a party of horsemen galloped along the valley and rode up to the crowd, which was increasing every moment. It was the emperor's suite, who, giving up all hope of following his perilous course, had gone back to where they had left their horses in the morning, and ridden round, hoping to meet their master on the other side of the mountain.

"Has the emperor passed this way?" one of them cried out. "He climbed up so far among the rocks that we lost sight of him."

The shepherd cast a terrified look at the wall, and pointing upward, said, "That must be he up yonder. God have mercy upon him!"

The emperor's attendants gazed at the figure, and at each other, in horror. One of them had a speaking-trumpet with him, such as mountaineers sometimes use for shouting to one another among the hills. He raised it to his mouth, and cried at the pitch of his voice, "If it is the emperor who stands there, we pray him to cast down a stone."

There was a breathless hush of suspense now among the crowd, and then down came the stone, crashing into the roof of a cottage at the foot of the rock.

A loud cry of lamentation broke from the people and was echoed on every side among the mountains. For they loved their young emperor for the winning charm of his manner, for his frank and kindly ways, and his especial fondness for their country.

The sound of that wail reached Maximilian's ears, and looking down, he could see the crowd of people, appearing from his giddy height like an army of ants—a black patch on the bright green of the valley. The sound and sight raised his hopes; he had completely given up all thought of delivering himself by his own exertions, but he still thought help from others might be possible. And now that his situation was discovered, the people he knew would do whatever lay in the power of man for his deliverance. So he kept up his courage and waited patiently and hopefully. It was so hard to believe that he, standing there in the bright sunshine, full of youthful health and strength, was a dying man and never would leave that spot alive.

Higher and higher rose the sun. It was midday now, and the reflected heat from the rocky wall was well-nigh too great to bear. The stones beneath his feet became hot as a furnace, and the sunbeams smote fiercely on his head. Exhausted by hunger and thirst, by heat and weariness, he sank down on the scorching rock. The furious headache and dizziness which came over him made him fear that he was about to become insensible. He longed for some certainty as to his fate before consciousness forsook him, and, following a sudden thought, he drew from his pocket a small parchment book, tore out a blank leaf and wrote on it with pencil, then tied the parchment to a stone with some gold ribbon he happened to have with him, and let the stone fall down into the valley as he had done the first. What he had written was the question, "Whether any human help was possible?" He waited long and patiently for the answer; but no sound reached his ear but the hoarse cry of the eagle. A second and a third time he repeated the message, lest the first should not have been observed—still there was silence, though the crowd in the valley had been increasing all day; and now a vast assembly—the inhabitants of Zierlein and all the district round—had gathered at the foot of that fatal throne which the emperor had desired for himself.

The day wore on; the sun was fast sinking toward the west, and Maximilian could no longer resist the conviction that there was no help possible, that all hope must be over for him. It seemed, as soon as he had faced this certainty, that a calm resignation, a high courage and resolve, took possession of his soul. If he was to die, he would die as became a king and a Christian—if this world were vanishing from him, he would lay firm hold of the next.

Again he tore a leaf from his book, and wrote on it. There was no more gold ribbon to bind it to the stone, so he took the chain of the Order of the Golden Fleece [in the medieval world, it was usually worn only by royalty]—what value had it for a dying man?—

and from that high and airy grave he threw the stone down among the living.

It was found, like the others before it. None had answered these, because no one was to be found willing to be a messenger of death to the much-loved emperor. The man who found the stone read the letter aloud to the assembled crowd, for the emperor's messages were addressed to all Tyrol.

And this was the last message:

"Oh, Tyrol, my last warm thanks to thee for thy love which has so long been faithful to me.

"In my pride and boastfulness I tempted God and my life is now the penalty. I know that no help is possible. God's will be done—His will is just and right.

"Yet one thing, good friends, you can do for me, and I will be thankful to you even in death. Send a messenger to Zierlein immediately for the Holy Sacrament, for which my soul thirsts. And when the priest is standing by the river, let it be announced to me by a shot, and let another shot tell me when I am to receive the blessing. And then I pray you unite your prayers with mine to the great Helper in time of need, that He may strengthen me to endure the pains of a lingering death.

"Farewell, my Tyrol,
Maximilian"

The reader's voice often faltered as he read this letter amid the sobs and cries of the multitude.

Off sped the messenger to Zierlein, and in all haste came the priest.

Maximilian heard the shot, and, looking down, could see the white robe of the priest standing by the river, which looked like a little silver thread to him. He threw himself on his knees in all penitence and submission, praying that he might be a spiritual partaker of Christ, though he could not receive in body the signs of salvation. Then the second shot rang on the air, and through the speaking-trumpet came the words of the blessing:

"May God's blessing be upon thee in thy great need—the blessing of the Father, the Son, and the Holy Ghost, whom heaven and earth praise for ever."

The emperor felt a deep peace filling his heart as the words of blessing were wafted to his ear.

The sun had by this time sunk behind the mountain range beyond the valley of Zierlein; but a rosy blush still lingered on the snowy summits, and the western sky glowed in crimson and gold. Beneath, in the deep purple shade of the valley, the people all knelt, and the emperor could hear a faint murmur, which told him they were praying for him.

Touched by their sympathy, he, too, continued kneeling in prayer for the welfare of his subjects.

It was quite dark now, and one by one the stars came forth on the deep blue sky, till at last all the heavenly host stood in glittering array. The sublime peace of those silent eternal fires stole in Maximilian's heart and drew his thoughts and desires heavenward to eternal Love and eternal Rest. So he knelt on, rapt in prayer and in lofty and holy thoughts.

Suddenly, a bright gleam flashed on his eyes, and a figure in a flicker and dazzle of light stood before him. No wonder that in his present mood, his spirit raised above earthly things, this vision should seem to him something more than human.

"Lord Emperor," it spake, "follow me quickly—the way is far, and the torch is burning out."

Hardly knowing whether he was still in the world of mortals or not, Maximilian asked, "Who art thou?"

"A messenger sent to save the emperor."

Maximilian rose; as he gazed, it seemed to him that the vision assumed the form of a bright-haired, barefooted peasant youth holding a torch in his hand.

"How didst thou find thy way to the cliff?" he asked.

"I know the mountains well, and every path in them."

"Has heaven sent thee to me?" asked Maximilian, still feeling as if he were in a dreamworld.

"Truly, it is God's will to deliver thee by my hand," was the simple answer.

The youth now turned and slid down into the hollow out of which Maximilian had climbed that morning, then glided through a crevice in the rock behind, which the emperor had failed to detect. Stooping low, he with difficulty squeezed through the narrow chink and saw the torch flaring below him, down a steep, rugged fissure which led into the heart of the rock. Leaping and sliding, he followed on, and the torch moved rapidly before him; its red light gleaming on metallic ores and glittering on rock crystals. Sometimes a low, thundering sound was heard, as of underground waterfalls, sometimes water, dripping from the rocky roof, made the torch hiss and sputter. Downward they went, miles and miles downward, till at last the ravine opened into a long, low, nearly flat-bottomed cavern, at the end of which the torch and its bearer suddenly vanished. But at the place where he had disappeared, there was a glimmer of pale light. Maximilian groped his way toward it, and drew a long breath as he found himself again in the open air, with the silent stars above him and the soft grass beneath his feet. He looked round for his deliverer, but no one was to be seen. He soon perceived that he was in the valley of Zierlein, and afar he heard a confused noise as of an assembled multitude. He followed the sound, but was forced to rest more than once from extreme weakness and weariness before he reached the foot of Saint Martin's Wall, and saw priest and people still kneeling in prayer for him. Deeply moved, he stepped into their midst and cried, "Praise the Lord with me, my people. See, He has delivered me!"

The emperor was never able to discover who had been the instrument of his wondrous rescue. A report soon spread among the people that an angel had saved him. When this rumor reached the emperor's ears, he said, "Yes, truly, it was an angel; my guardian angel, who has many a time come to my help."

Maximilian never forgot that day on Saint Martin's Wall. It taught him many a lesson. It is said that he never again went out chamois hunting without commending himself *a la garde de Dieu,* as the native mountaineers of Switzerland and Tyrol now are wont to do. And this spirit of thoughtless daring was sobered into a true and higher courage, which, throughout his life, never forsook him in the face of danger and death. ❧

We have been impressed, after much prayer, to include in this book a number of stories that can be validated by individuals in our own immediate family. It was exceedingly difficult to choose the story that would end up serving as the capstone of the collection, the one that brings the collection full circle from the lead story, Kirby Palmer's "The Turning Point." Only one story seemed perfect for the concluding story slot: Marla Palmer Marsh's "Let's Run Tell Our Friends"; for several reasons: it details an actual verified experience of what it might be like to see angels flying in the sky; what it would be like to see those heavenly beings be so conscious of the two girls that they remained directly above them until the girls came to a place of safety outside the dark woods; following that up with the sight of watching the angels fly away; and finally, note how the girls felt impelled to rush to the college campus and tell their friends about the experience.

It was a dark night on that heavily forested trail. Suddenly, a strange swishing sound—and when they looked up, they couldn't believe their eyes!

"Mama, is it *really* true you once saw angels?"

"Yes, dear, but haven't I told you the story before?"

"Well, yes, but never the full story. There has to be more to it than what you've told me. It's Friday evening, it has been a long hard week, and now, with a fire crackling in the fireplace, it's a perfect time for stories."

"All right, dear, but what do you mean by the 'full story'?"

"Oh, I don't know exactly, but why don't you take me back further in time than Howell Mountain days. Clear back to your childhood. You had a tough time of it, didn't you?"

"Well, yes. I can see why you think so, but we didn't think we were much worse off than most of our friends were. And with nine kids in the family, none of us had time to feel sorry for ourselves."

"*Nine* kids? Give me strength!"

"Oh, it wasn't that bad. There certainly was never a dull moment, however."

"Weren't you one of the younger ones?"

"Yes, next to the last. And Papa and Mama needed us all. After leaving the cotton fields of Texas, Papa moved us all to California, first southern and next central, where we planted, then hoed cotton. Goodness, it got hot in the San Joaquin Valley."

"What about school?"

"School? Oh my! Papa moved so often, I didn't get a full year in a classroom until my eighth grade. That's the way it went—until my blessed senior year; that year, I got to start in September and attend all year. Took two years of Spanish that year, doubled up with other classes too, for I didn't know if I'd ever be able to finish school if I didn't do it that year. And mighty few girls got to go to college back then. Papa certainly didn't have money to spare for such things."

"I don't understand, Mama, didn't you go on to college?"

"Oh, that's a miracle, Marla. As you know, my sister Flora and I were always very close. In fact, I'll never forget a Sabbath in Redlands, when I was fifteen—Flora and I were both baptized the same day."

"Flora. You've talked about her a lot through the years, haven't you? But, you haven't told me how the miracle happened."

"Oh yes, I can never forget that life-changing day. The very next Sabbath after our graduation, as Flora and I were talking to people after the service at the Hanford Adventist church, Mr. Hansen, a cattle rancher, walked up to us, and after small talk, asked what we were going to do with our lives now that we were out of school.

"I remember sighing, and saying we'd probably be just getting jobs and begin to make a living. Bless Mr. Hansen's heart, he must have seen something in us we didn't know was there, for he bored in and, looking first at me, then at Flora, asked if we had any plans to attend college.

"Flora and I were flustered, for that had long been our dream. We both hoped to become teachers someday. So we told Mr. Hansen that we'd dreamed of attending the Adventist college in the Napa Valley, but that was an utter impossibility!

"Mr. Hansen smiled, then dropped his bomb: 'Well, if you worked at Pacific Union College, and earned all you could, and I paid the rest, would you like to go?'

"Flora and I for so long had assumed such a thing to be impossible that we were all but speechless. When we finally realized the life-changing significance of his words, our joy gushed out in torrents. Of *course,* we'd jump at such an offer! We'd bless him until his dying day!"

"Mama! You'd never told me that story. And here we are today, taking college for granted. So what happened next?"

"Oh, we worked hard all summer, saving every penny we could. Come September, we packed up and made our way up to the Napa Valley; from St. Helena, we took the corkscrew road up Howell Mountain to Angwin; and there we found our college. We'd never seen such a beautiful place in all our lives! We'd spent most of our lives toiling in hot flat scorching farmland, and here was Pacific Union College, high on a mountain covered with oaks, evergreens, manzanita, madrones, and brush. We fell in love with it at once. For it made possible the rest of our lives." Then she smiled at her daughter, saying, "Without it, I'd never have had you, Connie, or Kirby."

"So what was college like, Mama?"

"Oh, it was wonderful! Quickly, Flora and I found work. We'd always worked hard, but now with the gift of a future, we worked even harder to justify Mr. Hansen's faith in us. And we learned far more than just book knowledge. And how we reveled in the beautiful music! From our fourth-floor room in Graf Hall—"

"Graf Hall? My old dorm?"

"The very same. So many wonderful memories are associated with that old dormitory. I'd started to say that, from our dorm window we could hear music—violin, piano, instrumental, vocal, wafting in our direction from the practice rooms. It just seemed like it was a little bit of heaven. And we loved our teachers."

"So where do angels come into the story?"

"Give me time to get to it. Don't rush me—you asked for the full story," laughed her mother.

"Sorry, take your time. I'm not trying to rush you. What happened next?"

"Well, after summer's work in the fields, we returned to PUC. But by that year, the Hansens were so invested in us that Mrs. Hansen moved from the San Joaquin Valley to a big farmhouse up on a hill north of the college. She invited Flora and me to stay with her and walk back and forth to the college, about a mile away. Back then, it was a lot wilder country than it is today, much more heavily forested, and many more wild animals—including mountain lions—than was true when you went to college there."

"Guess so, because I never saw a mountain lion during my college years there."

"Well, back to that second year—one could gain a teaching degree in only two years back then. Behind Mrs. Hansen's big farmhouse, a wide trail followed the ridge and eventually came out at a five-way intersection (one road went south to St. Helena, one west on White Cottage Road, one north to Pope Valley, one southwest down into the Napa Valley, and the fifth ascended a shady little hill, wandered through the entire college campus, and emerged at the south end of the hilltop crater).

"My, Flora and I loved those long walks through those gorgeous tall pine trees! Their fragrance in the wind—oh, they fed our souls! We walked that trail, early and late. I can remember how much fun it was to slip and slide on the pine needles."

"Ma-ma! Hard to believe you were ever that young!"

How her mother laughed! "I've not always been old, dear. In fact, I don't feel old even now. But back to that trail. It was great exercise too, after a heavy day of studying and work. Friday evenings and Sabbath mornings were the best, though, for then we could really enjoy the stroll. Of course, we had friends too, and would often spend time with them after classes or on Sabbath afternoons.

Glory One Friday Evening

"And now, dear, I come to the story you've been waiting for."

"I'd say, it's about time, were it not for your telling me, for the first time in my entire life, the larger story. Wouldn't have missed it for the world! But go on—"

"I can see that evening as though it was yesterday. I've thought so often, down through the years, about that never-to-be-forgotten experience. Flora and I have often wondered whether or not we were in danger that evening."

"From what?"

"Oh, I don't know. A mountain lion, perhaps. Someone lurking in the dark woods who meant us no good. We never came up with answers—only questions. All I can remember is that it was a dark Friday evening, before the moon lightened the sky. As we were walking along, each with our own thoughts, we heard a sound neither of us had ever heard before—a strange swishing sound. 'Pssst!' we hissed at each other. Though we listened intently, we couldn't see anything but the trees. But suddenly, we looked up: just above the pine trees were some bright white spots in the sky. We listened even more intently. It sounded like bird wings swishing. As we continued to watch, we could see faint outlines of large figures. As we waited, rooted to the ground in amazement, we could see figures going around in a circle. We've since debriefed many times and compared memories of that night. Both of us remember three groups of figures, and all three groups doing the same thing: turning in circles. But wait! The three circles were also moving in a larger circle—kind of like Ezekiel's wheel within a wheel. It was so curious. What were they? They were far too big to be birds. And they were doing things birds don't do—swishing their wings, turning in circles, and circles were going in circles too. I wonder . . . I WONDER IF THEY COULD BE ANGELS? WHAT ELSE COULD THEY BE?

"Suddenly, we both had the same thought: 'LET'S GO TELL OUR FRIENDS SO THEY CAN SEE THEM TOO!'

"We began to run. The angels moved too. We stopped. The angels stopped directly above us. Then we ran as fast as we could—the angels moved just as fast, remaining above us. We were now so excited, we ran out of the trees, out into the open, and down the steep trail to the five-way intersection. But alas! When we turned left to go up the campus road, the angels flew south, straight on down the St. Helena road—but slowly, not fast now, as they passed out over the valley and beyond.

"We were frozen there watching them leave us—until they were gone, never to be seen again. Then we ran to the dorm and excitedly told the story to our incredulous friends. And, as I told you, dear, Flora and I wondered and wondered why the angels showed themselves to us alone. Was there danger in the woods that night? If there was, most likely that enemy was as distracted and enthralled as we were—to such an extent they lost interest in attacking two young women on their way to vespers. I'm truly convinced, dear, that God sent His angels to protect us that night.

"But I won't know until Jesus tells us the rest of the story when we get to the kingdom."

Postscript:

One never-to-be-forgotten summer, when my mother and I were taking summer school classes at the college in Angwin, for the first and only time in my life, my mother told me the larger story, including the events that led up to her attending college at Pacific Union College. We even walked that same trail from which she and Flora saw the angels. Forever afterwards, she was convinced, beyond a shadow of a doubt, that God had a special plan for her life, a ministry uniquely her own. She felt called. ❧

ACKNOWLEDGMENTS

Introduction: "Is There a Difference Between Biblical and New Age Angel Stories?" by Joseph Leininger Wheeler. Copyright © 2013. Printed by permission of the author.

SECTION ONE

"The Turning Point," by Kirby Palmer. Copyright ©2013. Printed by permission of the author.

"Firewood and Candles," by W. A. Spicer. Published in Spicer's book *The Hand That Intervenes* (Washington, D.C.: Review and Herald® Publishing Association, 1918). Original text owned by Joe Wheeler.

"Angels in the Darkness," by Kari Surdahl. Copyright© 2002. Printed by permission of the author.

"The Master Controls the Switch," by Elna English Mays. Published in *The Youth's Instructor,* December 30, 1952. Reprinted by permission of Review and Herald® Publishing Association, Hagerstown, Maryland 21740. If

anyone can provide knowledge of the author or the author's next of kin, please relay to Joe Wheeler (P.O. Box 1246, Conifer, CO 80433).

"Guardian Angels," by Betty Jones. Published in *The Youth's Instructor,* October 31, 1950. Reprinted by permission of Review and Herald® Publishing Association, Hagerstown, Maryland 21740. If anyone can provide knowledge of the author or the author's next of kin, please relay to Joe Wheeler (P.O. Box 1246, Conifer, CO 80433).

"Hanging On by the Fingers," by Joseph Leininger Wheeler. Copyright © 2005. Printed by permission of the author.

SECTION TWO

"Through the Storm," by Mildred Wilson. Published in *The Youth's Instructor,* July 24, 1945. Reprinted by permission of Review and Herald® Publishing Association, Hagerstown, Maryland 21740. If anyone can provide knowledge of the author or the author's next of kin, please relay to Joe Wheeler (P.O.

Box 1246, Conifer, CO 80433).

"An Angel Walked," by Lois M. Parker. Published in *The Youth's Instructor,* February 18, 1958. Reprinted by permission of Review and Herald® Publishing Association, Hagerstown, Maryland 21740. If anyone can provide knowledge of the author or the author's next of kin, please relay to Joe Wheeler (P.O. Box 1246, Conifer, CO 80433).

"The Telegram That Saved My Train," author unknown. Published in *The Youth's Instructor,* August 19, 1924. Reprinted by permission of Review and Herald® Publishing Association, Hagerstown, Maryland 21740. If anyone can provide knowledge of the author or the author's next of kin, please relay to Joe Wheeler (P.O. Box 1246, Conifer, CO 80433).

"When Angels Rode Horseback," by Barbara Westphal. Published in *Junior Guide,* October 25, 1961. Reprinted by permission of Review and Herald® Publishing Association, Hagerstown, Maryland 21740. If anyone can provide knowledge of the author or the author's next of kin, please relay to Joe Wheeler (P.O. Box 1246, Conifer, CO 80433).

"John G. Paton and the Cannibals," by W. A. Spicer and John G. Paton. Published in Spicer's book *The Hand That Intervenes* (Washington, D.C.: Review and Herald® Publishing Association, 1918). Original text owned by Joe Wheeler.

"The Touch of Angel Hands," by Frances Daisy Duffie and Martha Duffie. Published in Marjorie Lewis Lloyd's book *It Must Have Been an Angel,* 1978. Reprinted by permission of Pacific Press® Publishing Association, Nampa, Idaho 83687. If anyone can provide knowledge of the author or the author's next of kin, please relay to Joe Wheeler (P.O. Box 1246, Conifer, CO 80433).

"Prayer and the Terror by Night," by Lieutenant Frank Lee. If anyone knows of the original publication, the author, or the author's next of kin, please relay to Joe Wheeler (P.O. Box 1246, Conifer, CO 80433).

SECTION THREE

"He Shall Give His Angels Charge Over You," by Lois Wheeler Berry. Copyright © 1998. Printed by permission of the author, Dorothy Johnson Muir, and Joe Wheeler.

"The Hand on the Wheel," by Deloris Bigler. Published in *The Youth's Instructor,* March 29, 1955. Reprinted by permission of Review and Herald® Publishing Association, Hagerstown, Maryland 21740. If anyone can provide knowledge of the author or the author's next of kin, please relay to Joe Wheeler (P.O. Box 1246, Conifer, CO 80433).

"Run!" by Josiah Litch. Published in W. A. Spicer's book *The Hand That Intervenes* (Washington, D.C.: Review and Herald® Publishing Association, 1918). Original text owned by Joe Wheeler.

"A Thousand Miles of Miracle," by A. E. Glover and W. A. Spicer. Published in Spicer's book, *The Hand That Intervenes* (Washington, D.C.: Review and Herald® Publishing Association, 1918). Original text owned by Joe wheeler.

"The Power of Song," by Nina Case. Published in *Stories Worth Re-Reading* (Washington, D.C.: Review and Herald® Publishing Association, 1919). Original text owned by Joe Wheeler.

"The Angels of Chortiza," by Gwendolen Lampshire Hayden. Published in *The Youth's Instructor,* May 6, 1952, as well as in Hayden's *Really Truly Stories,* book 7. Reprinted by permission of Review and Herald® Publishing Association, Hagerstown, Maryland 21740. If anyone can provide knowledge of the author or the author's next of kin, please relay to Joe Wheeler (P.O. Box 1246, Conifer, CO 80433).

SECTION FOUR

"The Calling Card," by Dixil L. Rodríguez. Published in *Adventist Review,* March 20, 2008. Reprinted by permission of the author and Review and Herald® Publishing Association, Hagerstown, Maryland 21740.

"Underneath," by Martin Pascoe. Published in *The Youth's Instructor,* April 6, 1937. Reprinted by permission of Review and Herald® Publishing Association, Hagerstown, Maryland 21740. If anyone can provide knowledge of the author or the author's next of kin, please relay to Joe Wheeler (P.O. Box 1246, Conifer, CO 80433).

"A Monarch's Restless Night," by W. A. Spicer. Published in Spicer's book, *The Hand That Intervenes* (Washington, D.C.: Review and Herald® Publishing Association, 1918). Original text owned by Joe Wheeler.

"Whiteout!" by Teresa Sales. Published in *Christian Reader,* November/December 1994. Reprinted by permission of the author.

"Providence in Revolution," by Ellsworth Schneider. Published in *The Youth's Instructor,* September 14, 1943. Reprinted by permission of Review and Herald® Publishing Association, Hagerstown, Maryland 21740. If anyone can provide knowledge of the author or the author's next of kin, please relay to Joe Wheeler (P.O. Box 1246, Conifer, CO 80433).

"Omnipresence," by Robert T. Jack. Published in *The Youth's Instructor,* September 28, 1948. Reprinted by permission of Review and Herald® Publishing Association, Hagerstown, Maryland 21740. If anyone can provide knowledge of the author or the author's next of kin, please relay to Joe Wheeler (P.O. Box 1246, Conifer, CO 80433).

"We Should Have Been Dead," by Marla Palmer Marsh. Copyright © 2013. Printed by permission of the author.

SECTION FIVE

"The Sea on My Back," by George Plume. If anyone knows of the original publication, the author, or the author's next of kin, please relay to Joe Wheeler (P.O. Box 1246, Conifer, CO 80433).

"Faith," by Mildred Hatch. Published in *The Youth's Instructor,* December 15, 1931. Reprinted by permission of Review and Herald® Publishing Association, Hagerstown, Maryland 21740. If anyone can provide knowledge of the author or the author's next of kin, please relay to Joe Wheeler (P.O. Box

1246, Conifer, CO 80433).

"Stop the Ship!" by W. S. Chapman. Published in *The Youth's Instructor,* April 21, 1914.

"God Will Take Care of You," by J. Echo Cossentine. Published in *The Youth's Instructor,* May 23, 1939. Reprinted by permission of Review and Herald® Publishing Association, Hagerstown, Maryland 21740. If anyone can provide knowledge of the author or the author's next of kin, please relay to Joe Wheeler (P.O. Box 1246, Conifer, CO 80433).

"The Mysterious Rider on PG-16," by Merton Henry Jr. Published in *The Youth's Instructor,* January 21, 1958. Reprinted by permission of Review and Herald® Publishing Association, Hagerstown, Maryland 21740. If anyone can provide knowledge of the author or the author's next of kin, please relay to Joe Wheeler (P.O. Box 1246, Conifer, CO 80433).

"Maximilian's Wish," author unknown. Published in Frank Leslie's *Popular Monthly,* 1876, volume 2. Original text owned by Joe Wheeler.

"Let's Run Tell Our Friends," by Marla Palmer Marsh. Copyright © 2013. Printed by permission of the author.